A Woman's Guide
to Making
Therapy Work

A Woman's Guide to Making Therapy Work

Joan Shapiro, M.D. and
Margaret Grant, M.D.

A BIRCH LANE PRESS BOOK
Published by Carol Publishing Group

A Birch Lane Press Book
Published by Carol Publishing Group
Birch Lane Press is a registered trademark of Carol Communications, Inc.
Editorial, sales and distribution, rights and permissions inquiries shuld be addressed to
Carol Publishing Group, 120 Enterprise Avenue, Secaucus, N.J. 07094
In Canada: Canadian Manda Group, One Atlantic Avenue, Suite 105, Toronto, Ontario
M6K 3E7

Carol Publishing Group books are available at special discounts for bulk purchases, sales
promotion, fund-raising, or educational purposes. Special editions can be created to
specifications. For details, contact: Special Sales Department, Carol Publishing Group,
120 Enterprise Avenue, Secaucus, N.J. 07094

Manufactured in the United States of America
10 9 8 7 6 5 4 3 2 1

Library of Congress Cataloging-in-Publication Data
Shapiro, Joan, 1950–
    A woman's guide to making therapy work / Joan Shapiro, Margaret
Grant.
        p.   cm.
    ISBN 1-55972-340-8 (hardcover)
    1. Women—Mental health,   2. Psychotherapy—Popular works.
3. Consumer education.   I. Grant, Margaret (Margaret Ellen)
II. Title.
RC451.4.W6S47   1996   95-50091
616.89'14'082—dc20   CIP

To our patients who teach us

Contents

Acknowledgments

We wish to acknowledge the patients with whom we have worked over the years who shared their lives and their journeys with us. We are honored to have worked with them.

We wish to thank the many colleagues (mostly women, but some unusual men) who have worked to make the new understanding of women into something concrete, real, and dynamic.

We wish to thank the members of the Denver Women's Psychiatrists' Study Group. Participating in this group inspired us to believe that our dream could be realized.

We wish to thank the staff of the Denver Women's Center, (especially Linda Lytle and Judy Hill, our original partners) who have made this whole endeavor so much richer an experience than just the two of us working together could ever have created. We also wish to include in our thanks the staff of the Women's Program at Mount Airy Psychiatric Center, especially Stephanie Lambert.

Specifically, we wish to thank Barbara Rainwater Redinger and George Hartlaub, who really believed in the project and who helped critique the manuscript and its ideas.

We wish to thank our agent, Faith Hamlin, for helping us shape this work into something better than we had imagined.

We wish to thank our editor, Jim Ellison, who, through his skill, helped us make sure we said what we really wanted to say.

From Joan:

For emotional and life support, my husband, George Hartlaub (whose feminism has been known to earn him the title of "honorary woman") is second to none. And I want to acknowledge the creative little person in my life, my daughter, Laura, who helps me think constantly about how it is to be a little girl growing up!

And, of course, I wish to thank Meg Grant, my partner for years in making a dream of something different for women into a reality.

From Meg:

Thanks to Nancy Cole and the staff of the Center for Trauma and Dissociation, who have used the chart presented in this book, given feedback, and helped to clarify its use.

To Joan for her love of writing, her willingness to work consistently on getting us toward our goal, and her insistence on meeting our deadlines.

To Alex and Laney, my children, for loving a mother who works on projects like this book more often than they would like. To Michelle Copeland for caring for them with such love while I am not available.

To my friends Martha Pearse, Barbara Rainwater Redinger, Sara Luther, and Elizabeth Bennett for being my friends and support. To my friend Jann Bass, who had me do her chart and many of her friends' charts on napkins in restaurants all over town.

Introduction

Being a therapist is exciting, fascinating, and rewarding. It is an awesome privilege to see someone open up, struggle, grow, and change. So it always strikes us as odd when someone says to us, "Oh, isn't it frustrating being a therapist?" or, "Don't you get tired of hearing the same thing, over and over again?" That isn't how we see it; for us it's a dynamic process.

When we started applying the most recent and sophisticated theories about the psychology of women, we had new tools that helped women progress faster. It helped, but not enough. Women still got stuck in their therapy. So we worked harder to pinpoint what is crucial to helping people get what they want out of life.

Of course, when most people come to therapy, they come because they are hurting and want to feel better. They don't *want* to get stuck. They want to use therapy to move ahead. They don't necessarily know how therapy actually works, and although they come with hope and need and good intentions, without some good information and understanding about how therapy works, all their hard work and good intentions may not pay off. Too often, how therapy works remains a mystery and leaves patients frustrated and confused. We think that understanding the therapeutic process is vital to a dynamic therapy and a successful outcome, and we propose to give you that understanding.

In order to make your therapy a success, you have to focus your energy and attention on (1) what the real problems are and (2) what you can really change. It's as simple as that.

And yet not so simple; the human mind is a complicated and wonderful thing. Its main instincts are to make us feel happy and safe and to keep us from feeling pain and fear. It will do almost anything to keep us from feeling pain, even if feeling that pain is the important first step toward true healing and ultimate happiness. In the process of protecting us from this pain, our mind ends up creating problems that are worse than the ones we were trying to avoid. The result is a new kind of pain.

So, although the strategy to make therapy effective is simple (work on what you really can change), it becomes complicated by the mind's natural tendency to protect us from pain, thus keeping us from the essential task. What we need, then, is a way to override this automatic protection plan and to substitute a conscious healing plan.

To do this, you will need two things: (1) a willingness to question your automatic beliefs and (2) a willingness to go through some temporary pain in order to experience permanent relief. If you accept those two ground rules, we can help you.

In this book, we will show you how to understand and take control of your own automatic emotional defenses, and how to direct your hard work so that you will get the kind of change that you want to achieve. We will do this in three steps: First, we'll explain how the mind works to set up these defenses. Next, we'll show you how to recognize when these defenses get you off track. And finally, we will give you a simple technique to help you stay in charge of your own process of change.

Although anyone can benefit from this guide, we direct it toward women because women's psychological defenses interfere with therapy in specific ways. We have worked with thousands of women in our clinic—the Denver Women's Center—and we see these defenses in operation every day. So this book addresses how to make therapy work from a woman's perspective.

If you are in therapy now, this guide will help you focus your work. If you are contemplating therapy, it will help clarify how therapy can help you. Either way, using the simple strategies in this book will help you maximize your efforts and your results.

Everything that we are going to suggest to you has worked for real women in therapy. We have been privileged to participate with these women in their healing processes, and watching them change has helped us clarify the principles we will present to you. Their stories make up a good deal of this book. Although their experiences and their work are real, the women described in this book are either composites or disguised versions of real women.

So let us begin with one of these women, Kathy. Let us use her story to guide you through your own.

Part I

The Problems

— 1 —

If You Love Me, I'll Feel Better

Kathy was very unhappy. Like many people, she thought she had everything she could want in life, so why did she feel so bad?

Hers was a picture-perfect kind of beauty, the kind that seems natural and effortless. Her skin was clear and radiant, her hair, in its short, simple style, looked healthy and shiny and always freshly trimmed. Because she was slim and athletic-looking, she looked good in whatever she wore.

Her husband was a handsome and successful business executive. He had participated in the growth and success of his new company, and his salary and job security were both high.

Her two children were as adorable as she. They were properly spaced and happily placed in school. Their lovely and spacious home was in one of the best neighborhoods, and the public schools there were outstanding.

Everything was in place. With such a fortunate life, she should feel satisfied. She concluded that there must be something wrong with her if she couldn't make herself feel okay. The more she fought her unhappiness, the larger and more constant it became in her life. She had to make the pain go away.

She began to stay up late at night drinking wine and watching TV. She found that she couldn't sleep unless she drank herself into a stupor. It wasn't that she was an alcoholic, she figured, since no one was ever around when she was drinking. So she assumed that her being drunk didn't affect her or her family.

Of course, she forgot that each morning she would be hungover and grouchy, and that her constant drinking made her depressed. She was unaware of how her drinking interfered with her sleep, and that this added to her stress.

She had given up her career to care for her two children. She had always intended to go back to work. But the longer she stayed away, the less confident she became about being able to be successful again. Besides, her husband's career was going very well; there was no need for a second income. And with her not working, it was easier for her to move if he got a promotion and a transfer. So she found lots of reasons to put off resuming a career. The longer she postponed it, the lower her self-esteem became.

She focused more and more on her appearance and began losing weight. With so many things feeling out of control, at least she could control this. She developed bulimia, in secret, of course, while her husband was at work and her children were at school.

But none of these problems was severe enough for her to think about entering therapy. In fact, she thought it was ungrateful and selfish of her to be so unhappy. The suicidal thoughts she had, though, scared her. Even she could recognize that these thoughts were not normal.

And so began Kathy's long venture into psychiatric treatment. In her therapy, she talked about her addiction to alcohol, her depression, her eating disorder, her low self-esteem, her sense of helplessness, her uselessness. She stopped drinking, she took anti-depressant medication, and she was hospitalized in an eating disorders program to deal with her bulimia. In these various therapies, she looked at her family and marital issues. She worked in therapy for years. And she kept coming up with the same thing: she was the problem. She was weak, selfish, unmotivated, and basically not a very valuable human being. She could find no other source for all of her sadness and her mental turmoil. Her children were well behaved and adorable, and her husband was a gem. Her father had been fun-loving and involved, and her mother had been steady, loving, and available. When she was growing up, she was considered morose and troublesome. Both her brother and sister were well adjusted, corroborating for Kathy her sense that there was no family problem to be addressed as a source of her problems. No, it was just her.

But isn't psychotherapy supposed to help someone with problems like Kathy's to feel better? If Kathy was in therapy for years, then why *wasn't* she much better? And what hope is there for people like Kathy? Are they simply going to be wasting their time, money, and hope?

That depends on what they do in their therapy. Let's look at what Kathy worked on—and why that didn't help.

Kathy dealt primarily with her bad feelings about herself. She didn't really know how therapy was supposed to help her. But she believed that if she talked to this skilled professional about her bad feelings, then, somehow, they would eventually go away. So, she talked about how bad she was, and her therapist would reassure her that this wasn't so, trying to put her feelings in perspective.

She liked her therapist, and she felt good with him. For forty-five minutes a week, she felt valuable and important. She kept hoping that this good feeling would stick with her. If she just sat with him long enough, maybe she would change or if she could just get him to love her enough, maybe she would feel better.

All along, Kathy maintained that she came from a normal background and had had an uneventful childhood. That was no lie. Kathy was not trying to deceive herself or her therapist. She really believed there was nothing to work on there. She just had to work on herself, and try to feel better.

Then Kathy's husband got a promotion and a transfer to open a branch office of his company. She had to start all over with a new therapist. A woman this time. This new therapist got the same history of a wonderful, problem-free family life, but because of the way Kathy glossed over her history as so completely uneventful, the therapist confronted Kathy as to whether this was completely true. She pushed Kathy a little to find a clue to what the family problems might have been. The confrontation marked the beginning of change.

One day, Kathy came in looking almost like a different person. She seemed optimistic, articulate, even energetic, and she began talking about her father's illegal business dealings. They hadn't exactly been a secret; she hadn't repressed them. She just hadn't thought of them as any kind of a problem. But, in fact, they had been a problem, because all of the children had had to lie to cover up some of their father's shady transactions.

So, her father wasn't perfect after all. That was a bit of a shock for Kathy, and she didn't like it. But she noticed that after she accepted it, she began to feel better. The reality about her father was painful and disappointing, but it was tolerable. And her perspective about herself had shifted. She felt a little hopeful, with a welcome infusion of energy.

However, she couldn't stay with it. In the next session, she was back to her old self. She was depressed again and full of self-blame. The issue about her father was irrelevant, she said. Her father was wonderful, her family was wonderful—she herself was the problem.

Back and forth she went. As she uncovered more disturbing truths about her family, she would have periods of real aliveness, energy, and optimism. As long as she dealt with the reality, she showed improvement. But she resisted staying in that place. Her old fantasies about her perfect family kept taking over because she wanted them back. And when they did she felt like her old self—worthless and miserable—and she wanted her therapist to help her with *that* reality.

Like most people in therapy, she wanted to feel better. She wanted to have a greater sense of self-esteem, more happiness, better relationships, and more appreciation from others. But she wanted to feel better while maintaining her beliefs about her own badness and unlovability. And, in a way, she expected all of this to happen simply by being in a healing presence, as though she could be filled up with self-esteem at a tank. She could tell her therapist her problems, and she would get better.

This didn't work, because *she* wasn't actually changing anything. She didn't want to have to give up anything in order to get those good things. Yes, she wanted to get rid of her depression and self-hatred, but not her fantasy of a perfect family. She didn't realize that that was exactly what she would have to give up in order to find true empowerment.

Another fantasy interfered with her getting well—a common one. She thought that her therapist would somehow find the magic key to a secret, or would give her a magic pill, or would just by being there, somehow figure out what was wrong and fix her.

Truly, her therapists were kind, and that is an important factor in the healing process. But what we do with that kindness is what is important because, in itself, kindness soothes, but it does not create change. The therapist can be a key facilitator but must be so in very concrete ways, such as by helping the client learn new patterns of behavior, by helping the client draw a map of where to go, and by helping the client separate the past from the present. The therapist can help as a companion or a coach on a long journey, and be there as a support during grieving.

This can be a very different kind of relationship—and one grounded in reality, not in fantasy. It can be a relationship with someone who cares enough to challenge your beliefs, and who, as your cheerleader, says, Yes, you *can* feel better. But it is not a fantasy relationship with someone whose mere presence will make everything okay. That belief is a trap.

Kathy's new therapist dared her to face the truth. That new therapist—Margaret Grant—began to draw a chart for her, to help her see that when she believed the fantasies, she paid a big psychological price. When she believed reality, on the other hand, she could be herself and reach out for happiness.

Kathy had to work on very difficult issues, including the painful reality that her father had sexually abused her, and that she had appeared depressed and morose to everybody in the family because she had been traumatized. Facing those tragedies allowed her to begin building her self-esteem, and to make plans for her future.

What Kathy did differently in her second, successful therapy was to face pain that she'd thought she could not tolerate. All of us need help and support to face this pain. We hope to provide a piece of that help and support in this book.

We often need a therapist to get us through a reality that otherwise seems too painful. Looking back at the traumas, losses, and disappointments of childhood, it is a natural response to block them out and pretend they never existed or that they don't matter very much. But they continue to have an effect on us, even while we are denying their reality or importance. Having a therapist to accompany us on a painful journey can give us the courage to stick with the painful reality and to try not to block it out in order to move beyond it.

A book, of course, is not a replacement for good therapy. But a book can be a guide, a cheerleader, and a positive force that says, "Yes, you can do it," and, "Yes, it is worth it."

Our intention in this book is to tell you what happens in therapy. How therapy works often seems mysterious. Because of this, patients often don't know what questions they should ask or how they should help guide the therapy in order to get what they want. We will explain what a therapist can (and can't) do for you and help you to judge whether you have the therapist who's right for you.

We will also describe the common roadblocks that exist to getting what you want in therapy. We will tell you how these issues affect women in particular, as we discuss ways of approaching relationships.

Next, we are going to provide you with the chart that Dr. Grant made for Kathy. We challenge you to use it. In making your own chart, you will be expected to do some demanding work. You will be asked to name *your* fantasies (and we'll explain in greater detail, as we go on, exactly what we mean by this), and the pain you would feel if those fantasies weren't true. You will also be asked to name the symptoms you want to get rid of. And, finally (this part can be very difficult for many people) you should be ready to name your positive qualities, to say who you really are when you are being all you can be.

These questions and rules present many difficulties, and so this chart won't be easy to make—just as therapy isn't easy. But we ask you to look at it as a special support to give you courage to face your fears and your pain. Nobody wants to face them. But we are confident that if you take this risk you will discover that you can do much more than you ever thought you could. You will have made real progress in achieving your goals by creating the changes that you want and need in your life.

— 2 —

I Want to Feel Better, But Don't Make Me Change

How many psychiatrists does it take to change a lightbulb?
One, but the lightbulb has to really want to change.

The Chinese word for crisis is a combination of two characters meaning "danger" and "opportunity." Most of us don't take enough advantage of opportunity; instead, seeing only danger, we do our best to avoid crisis. When it comes, and we get pushed to our limit, we are *forced* to change.

A friend of ours, Sandy, was struggling to balance family and her career as a management trainer and consultant. Both were important to her, and she didn't know what to give up in order to feel more satisfaction. Her husband had a well-paying job, and they could manage without her salary indefinitely. But if she slowed down her career in such a competitive field, she was afraid she wouldn't be able to pick it up again. She loved her work and she was quite talented. On the other hand, if she didn't spend more time with her children, she and they would miss that crucial time together forever. And one of her children, a boy, was having some adjustment problems that needed extra attention and energy. She knew that more attention from her and her husband now would have big payoffs in their son's future. She was at a loss as to what to do.

What finally forced her decision? She suffered a recurrence of an old back injury and had to have emergency surgery. With a long recuperation requiring her to limit her activities, she decided to put her career on hold until both children were in the first grade. Another option would have been to get into family therapy, encourage her husband to spend more time with the children, hire a full-time nanny, and focus more on her career.

The issue here is not the choice that Sandy made, but that she waited until she was forced to make one. She changed her life and is now happier. But she had been unable to make that change for herself. No matter how much dissatisfaction and anxiety she was feeling in her life, it was more frightening for her to change it than to simply soldier on.

In this example, Sandy was forced to make a very concrete change in her life. Psychological change is very similar to lifestyle change. For example, no matter how much pain and frustration we may feel from relentlessly trying to get the recognition we wish we had received from a parent, we keep on trying. To change would mean to stop this pursuit, and *giving up the struggle seems more risky than continuing it.* And so we go on and on, doing what we are doing, hoping it will eventually work, and suffering the consequences.

This has been the issue for Pam, a feisty, energetic little person with a big zest for life. The oldest child and the only daughter in a large working-class family, Pam was pushed aside at an early age so that her mother could care for the younger children. Very soon, she became her mother's helper, caring for a quick succession of younger brothers.

As in many families, and in most cultures around the world, Pam's family valued boys more than girls. Boys could carry on the family business; boys could achieve great things in academics and in sports, and they could make the family proud. No one expected much of girls, and not much was expected of Pam, out in the world. But in the home, her job was to be helpful and cooperative, and she was to be well-behaved and attractive at all times.

It didn't take long for Pam's mother to feel overwhelmed. The child of a strict and unaffectionate home herself, she did not handle the needs of many small children well. She was easily angered, and she expressed her anger quickly, with cutting comments and quick slaps with the back of a hand.

Many children in such situations learn to be compliant and quiet, and then deal with the consequences of this strategy later on in life. But Pam chose a different route. Because she had never gotten enough love and attention in the first place, she was not ready (or able?) to give up on trying to get it, no matter what the consequences. Even though her mother believed Pam's attention-seeking behavior was demanding and difficult, and often threatened to send her away if she didn't behave, Pam kept trying to win her love.

Now, thirty years later, what is happening to Pam? To put her problems in context, you have to know her a little better. She is strong, intelligent, and articulate. She has a big, sensitive heart, and is capable of great commitment. With a master's degree in her profession, she brings those talents to her work and is very much appreciated. She's also very funny.

But Pam's unsuccessful struggle to win her mother's love (in the form in which she feels she still needs it) has been costly. She doesn't see herself as she really is, but rather in terms of that struggle. For one thing, her self-esteem is low. She has a serious problem with bingeing (she has a diagnosable eating disorder, in fact), which probably originated as a reaction to her mother's withholding of food because she thought that Pam was too heavy. In any group, she never feels as though she really belongs. She gets depressed easily and often (although her energy and strength keep her going). She wants to have close friends, but is rarely open enough about herself to experience much real intimacy or safety in a relationship. *And she is still fighting for her mother's love.*

Pam is afraid to change how she looks at herself and the world because she is afraid to give up the fight. To her, it means that she will never get what she wants from her mother. It is too painful to admit that she never got what she needed from her in the first place. She comes to therapy wanting to change: she wants to stop overeating; she wants to be less depressed; she wants to feel like she belongs somewhere, and she wants to establish meaningful relationships.

Those are the changes she wants to make. But like so many of us, she resists changing what she believes is necessary in order to survive. She doesn't know that she is seeking the impossible. She realizes that she wants to feel better about herself, but she hasn't accepted what she will have to do to accomplish this: She will have to give up the fight. She will have to give up the dream that someday she will be able to get her mother to love her in the ways she has always wanted her to.

Pam's mother was tired and overwhelmed and had a limited amount to give. (We could speculate, too, that there was a mismatch between Pam's and her mother's basic temperaments, with Pam craving a more intense, immediate connection than her mother wanted or could have with Pam.) Whatever the cause, it is likely that Pam didn't get what she wanted from her mother because of issues that had to do with her mother, not with her. Yet Pam has judged her lovability and worth by the amount of love her mother could give her.

If Pam wants to feel better about herself and be loved better, she will have to see that *she* was never unlovable. The only way for Pam to do this is to recognize the truth about what her mother could give her. (She will have to give up the fantasy she created in her childhood about the bad girl with the loving mother.) She will have to learn to love herself and to turn to others who are better at loving. It's a formidable task, and it is the kind of task for which most of us have very few skills when we come to therapy, though these skills are exactly what therapy can help us acquire.

Pam certainly doesn't think of her struggle to win her mother's love as optional. In fact, her struggle has become a part of her identity. She can't even imagine who she would be if she were not discouraged and depressed. This is the way life is, and this is the way she is. She can't imagine changing it. She just doesn't want her struggle to make her feel so bad, and she wants to be able do it better, *so it will work!*

That's what usually happens when we go into therapy. "Help me feel better," we tell the therapist, but "don't make me change," we tell ourselves.

If You Love Me, I'll Feel Better

A part of each of us, like Peter Pan, won't grow up. And that part is still working on some unfinished business from childhood, trying to make the past into something that it is not. In a way, it's not as if that part of us won't grow up; it's that it won't *give* up and is still trying like crazy to make something work out right. It's amazing that we humans are so tenacious when it comes to creating what we want for ourselves out of life. However, we often don't have the creativity of a rat in a maze, who, when he finds out there is no cheese at the end of one path, tries another one. We just keep looking in the same place. As adults, we think if we try harder, or do it the same way but better, or make ourselves more deserving, then this time we will finally be rewarded. We are this blind and stubborn because we are doing something we learned when we were young and when there *weren't* any good choices. There was only a maze with no cheese at the end.

The reward we have been looking for since childhood is usually adult love and approval. Some of us become virtual junkies for this kind of approval; no matter how much we get, it's never enough. But all of us need some, and that need often comes from the small child within us that wants more of it.

This is not to say that we have this leftover need because all parents are poor parents. One parent's care and attention can never (and, it is argued by some experts, should never) match a child's emotional needs perfectly.

So, here we are, adults on the outside, but on the inside, a part of us feels that if someone only loves us enough, then every-thing will be okay, and we will be soothed. How natural, then, for us to seek this love from a therapist. And for some problems, that is all that is needed. With some support to add confidence, we can often come up with solutions to our own problems.

But sometimes, this natural tendency to want more love and support backfires on us. For example, we may see ourselves as the small child and the therapist as the "big person," all-knowing, all-powerful, the one with the right answers, the one who can make us all better. This stance, appropriate for a child in need of adult nurturing, disempowers an adult. With the wish for someone else to fix us often comes the relinquishment of our own inner resources.

This certainly has been true for Pam. Although she is very bright, very knowledgeable about psychology, and competent and accomplished in most areas of her life, therapy has become a mixed bag for her. Her therapist's warmth, support, and under-standing help her flourish and move forward, take risks, and grow. But Pam also gets trapped by her therapist's caring and attention. Could this be the love that she has been looking for?

By seeing her therapist as the one and only, the substitute for her mother's missing love, Pam gets derailed. She thinks that this therapist's love is special and unique, like a mother's love. Her therapist, in fact, likes her in the same ways that anyone else would like her, because whether she knows it or not, Pam is a very likable person. So this is no great accomplishment on the part of the therapist! It is true that the therapist understands her better than anyone else ever has. Well, why not? Pam has told her more and trusted her with more than she has trusted anyone else. And the therapist is trained to understand and make sense out of otherwise confusing thoughts and feelings.

The problem in this therapy is that Pam attributes extra-ordinary qualities to the therapist. She ends up feeling that she is loved because the therapist has a special capacity to love, not because she is lovable. All of the power to heal rests with the therapist, and none of it with Pam. Pam wants to maintain good feelings between herself and her therapist, and she becomes too focused on the relationship as an end in itself, rather than as a vital tool.

Pam's response to being in therapy is not uncommon. We come to depend on the goodwill and even love of this person who is supposed to help us. But although goodwill is an essen-tial part of healing, it is far from enough. Yet this childlike part of us acts as if the goal is to be loved by the therapist as we wish to be loved by everyone else. If we can gain this kind of love, we will naturally feel better. It is as if whatever is wrong with us will be fixed if this special person likes us.

With the idea that someone else is bigger and better than we and can love us into emotional health comes an inevitable sense of powerlessness. From this stance, the therapist is not an ally or a coach. She is the one with the answers, the insight, and the healing. She is a savior. When we are hurting and in need, it is comforting to think that someone can save us. But we give up an awful lot to get that kind of omnipotent help: we give up our-selves. We are in a position of passivity and expectancy. From this position, we are unlikely to see ourselves as agents of our own change or as unique human beings, full of resources. Instead, we see ourselves as being inadequate, needy, and pow-erless, and we are grateful that we are with someone who, thank-fully, is powerful.

But we didn't come to therapy to become powerless, did we? We came to become powerful, confident, and secure. But when we enter psychotherapy, that needy childlike part of us gets accessed almost instantly. This is often referred to as transference—the idea that our feelings and certain patterns from our past relationships get "transferred" onto someone else in the present. If we are aware of it, we can understand it, use it, and work with it. If we are unaware of it, then it gains control over us. And a situation that is supposed to enhance our self-esteem and capabilities can turn into one in which we depend on someone else to supply them for us.

A cultural reality also contributes to our giving up control when we go for help. The sense that someone who is bigger and more powerful than we will fix things for us is supported by the medical model of treatment. We learn by going to doctors that someone else will decide what is wrong, make the decisions, and prescribe the cure. We bring this cultural belief into psychotherapy, too.

For example, if we go to a dentist to cure a toothache, the dentist will probably do something to us. We will lie in the chair and be worked on. All that is required of us is that we allow the dentist to do his job. On the other hand, if we go to a voice coach to learn how to sing, the coach will listen to us, make suggestions, and give us exercises. But the coach can't make us into a better singer. We, ourselves, are the agent, and the improvement in our voice depends on the work we do.

The medical model leads us to behave as though we are going to the dentist. But going to a psychotherapist is more like going to the voice coach: we do the work.

As little children, there was a big person who could soothe us, and whose love and presence could make everything all better. But psychotherapy is different: that kind of instant cure is not possible. Someone else isn't the savior. We use a caring expert's help, but the person who saves us is ourselves.

The Relational Self

All these issues are particularly hazardous for women. In our culture, we are trained from infancy to be the emotional caretakers. We learn to empathize and to anticipate the emotional needs of others. It's as though if everybody else feels good, then we know that we have done our job. (Does that sound like a job that is ever done?) We learn about who we are by how success-ful we are in relationships.

This has been called a woman's "relational self" and has been written about by Carol Gilligan, Jean Baker Miller, and oth-ers at the Stone Center at Wellesley. A woman gets a sense of who she is within, and gets defined by, her relationships. This means that for us as women to feel good about ourselves, we have to feel good about our relationships. Unlike men, who are more likely to define themselves by what they do or by their accomplishments, we tend to define ourselves by how we get along with others. Often, then, as a result, we want everyone—including a therapist—to like us.

So women are doubly likely to end up feeling that therapy is about getting a therapist to like them. First, the natural child-hood need for love comes out, along with the hope that another person who loves you enough can make everything better. Then comes the relational style—the tendency to work on relation-ships as if they are the self. Turning therapy into the project of getting a therapist's love is hardly a surprising outcome for women. Many women spend a lot of energy in therapy trying to keep the therapist happy.

"How Can I Help You?"

The classic Freudian style of doing psychotherapy, which many psychotherapists bring to their work, can also contribute to pas-sivity, to the tendency to "wait" for relief to come. This technique involves waiting for the patient to bring things up, rather than initiating discussions in the therapy. The theory behind this tech-nique is quite sound, and much of it comes out of Freudian or psychoanalytic theory. The therapy is about the client, about her needs, priorities, perspectives, and conflicts. If the therapist were to start the session, pick a topic, or suggest what should be worked on, this could, potentially, say more about the therapist and less about what the client thinks is important.

For example, perhaps a woman asks for help with anxiety. She is unhappy both at work and at home. Deep down, she senses that her home life is extremely problematic, and if she felt the support and love of her husband, she would be less stressed at work. But the therapist thinks that by struggling so much at work, she is burning the candle at both ends. Of course her home life is suffering. She arrives home every day feeling exhausted and unappreciated. She has nothing left to deal with otherwise normal issues at home.

Neither perspective is right or wrong. But one is the client's, the other is the therapist's. Since this is the client's therapy, the therapist will want to be careful not to direct it with what may simply be her own personal bias. That is the value in a non-directive approach. In addition, if the client is too passive and expects the therapist to know what is important, the client's real feelings and priorities may be neglected.

It's also important for the client to learn to feel free to bring up whatever comes to mind and whatever is important to her. If the therapist leads the discussion, the client can end up molding her thoughts and responses to fit what she believes the therapist expects or approves of.

Sometimes the client needs the therapist to be a "blank screen" onto which she can project issues and feelings from her own life and relationships so that she can more vividly experience them. In order for this to happen, the therapist must sometimes be neutral enough for these transfers of feelings to occur. That is another reason for the therapist to hang back a little and let the client take the lead. (The issue of transference will be dealt with in more detail in chapter seven.)

For these reasons, then, the therapist may refrain from giving direction and may assume the client will determine the direction. Sometimes this works well. But sometimes, if the client is especially passive, or comes with a strong desire to find a savior, or a strong impulse to avoid painful feelings, this technique can get in the way. The therapist expects the client to say what she wants fixed, and the client expects the therapist to fix her—and both can be politely waiting for each other. Not much change is going to occur in this atmosphere. Without knowing how or why change is supposed to occur, the client is simply waiting for it to happen.

Waiting and hoping to feel better or expecting someone else to fix us are approaches that make change unlikely. Thinking that getting the right person to love us will make us finally feel good about ourselves is another strategy that will not work and that will ultimately rob us of our own self-worth. Perhaps the biggest roadblock to change is the fear of addressing the pain in our lives. We are all afraid to make the decision to change.

For Pam, the decision to change came when some of her symptoms got worse despite the work she thought she was doing in therapy. Just being there clearly wasn't enough. Her therapist's supportive words weren't enough. Being a "good patient" by being cooperative and interesting certainly wasn't enough. Even learning about her past and how that past affected her in the present wasn't enough. But she was aware from her work in therapy that her symptoms meant something.

With the help of her therapist, she began to revisit some of the themes in her life: her distant father and, especially, her critical mother. The old pain came back almost unchanged. Was she really still waiting for her mother to love her? How could this be? After all, hadn't she already "dealt with" these issues?

She had, in fact, worked on them quite a bit, but her work always had a piece of denial attached to it. Whenever the bad feelings from her childhood came along, she blamed herself for feeling so bad, decided that what had happened couldn't really have been so painful, and that she was just overly sensitive. Then she could push the feelings away, and by blaming herself she could, in effect, dismiss them as invalid. By doing this, she never really grieved over that pain from her childhood. And of course it came back again and again, but in the form of symptoms of depression and low self-esteem. She looked to her therapist to soothe her, and this worked temporarily. But since the pain she felt about being a bad person wasn't the underlying problem, nothing changed.

This time, she worked not to push away the real pain. She heard her therapist more clearly when her therapist pointed out how she was trying to dismiss that pain. This was the real work of her therapy. It wasn't about feeling good, or getting along with her therapist, or about having her therapist be able to *do* something because of her professional skill. It was about *Pam* making the change and allowing herself to feel the pain.

Pam found the courage to do this work once she understood that the pain of handling her feelings in the same old way was worse than the pain of facing what was painful in her childhood. It is that same perspective we want you to gain by reading this book and by working on your issues in the ways we suggest. This change is very hard work, and you need whatever technical assistance and support you can get.

Kathy, the woman presented in Chapter One, was caught much like Pam. Kathy was a very "good" patient. She never missed an appointment. She talked openly about all of her symptoms. She participated in an alcohol treatment program, and she took her medication as prescribed. This all fit with Kathy's coping style, the strategy she learned as a child: if I'm good and I don't upset anyone, then I will be accepted, and things will be okay. But being good in this way protected her from her pain and prevented her from coming to grips with her real problems.

Her therapist helped her see that when she was facing, rather than denying, the most difficult things in her life, she was most like the person she wanted to be (energetic, creative, and alive). But when she was denying the very real pain, her symptoms (depression, anxiety, etc.) appeared immediately, and unchanged.

Like Pam, and like all of us, she didn't want to face that real pain. So she used all of her lifelong habits and psychological defenses to protect herself from this pain. Naturally, then, she followed the same pattern in therapy. "Help me feel better, but don't make me change," could be translated into, "Please take away the pain, but don't make me feel it." Unfortunately, the only way to end the pain is to go through it, and, of course, we all try our hardest not to have to go through it.

Fears and defensive strategies like Pam's and Kathy's, are natural, but they interfere with getting meaningful results out of therapy. They are also not obvious when they are occurring; they are part of our everyday view of the world and have been with us for a long time. This makes them very difficult to see. In the next chapter, we will describe what these strategies might look like so that you can recognize them for what they are and can work with them as part of the process of change.

Clearly, Pam and Kathy had to do a lot of work to be able to confront their pain. It is not a simple or an easy process, and it takes time as well as work. But knowing how the process works and how to think about goals for therapy will give you a much greater chance for success.

— 3 —

Why Don't We Let Someone Help Us?
Our Love Affair With Fantasy

A Fairy Tale

Once upon a time, there was a little girl named Mary. She lived in a house with her mother and her father and a pet cat named Whiskers. Mary was a sweet and pleasant child. She had a very cute smile and a pretty singing voice. Her teachers liked her, and she had a best friend who lived on the other side of town. She had her own room with lots of stuffed animals and her very own easel with a chalkboard on one side.

But there was trouble in her house. On payday, her father would spend his money at the local bar on the way home, so there was always a shortage of food at the end of the month. Mary didn't mind because she liked to eat oatmeal, even for supper. But her mother would get very angry, and it wouldn't be any fun to play at home. Her mother and father would yell at each other. When that happened, Mary would go upstairs and talk to Whiskers. Or she would go outside and play make-believe in the tall bushes that grew beside their house.

23

She would play two games. In one, she was really a princess and would someday return to her true home. That was fun, but it was so unreal that it didn't help for long. No matter how much she thought about having a wonderful king and queen as parents, and a wonderful castle to live in, she always ended up in this family.

The other game she would play was different. In this game, Mary would try to figure out what was wrong with her and then how to fix it. She thought of all the things she could do better, she thought of all the mistakes she had made that day, and she thought of all the ways she could keep from making those mistakes again. She was able to think of a lot of things that might stop her mom and dad from fighting.

She could get an A instead of A− on her next spelling test. That would help. They would be so proud of her. She could keep the cat from scratching the furniture. (That would be nice, but she didn't know if she could ever control Whiskers that much.) She could not ask for seconds when there wasn't enough food. She could be more pleasing to her daddy so that when he came home he would be happy instead of angry.

This last one was hard to figure out because you never knew when daddy was going to get angry, so you never knew what was wrong, and you never knew exactly what would please him. But she could make sure that when he got home she was clean, that her hair was combed, and that she had helped mommy in the kitchen. She could make sure that the newspaper was ready for him to read, that she brought home good grades, and that she never had noisy friends at the house (well, *all* her friends were noisy, so she could play at their houses). And she could always smile at daddy. Maybe all of that would help keep him in a good mood.

And there were things she could do for mommy. She could stay out of her way when she was cooking. It always made her grouchy if Mary asked her questions when she was busy in the kitchen. She could set the table and do the dishes every day. She could keep her room clean—mommy liked it when things were clean. She could pay attention when something bothered mommy and try to make her happy again.

This second game kept her occupied for hours at a time, because there was so much to think about. And she could keep playing it for real. She had so many ideas about how to make things better. If she did all the right things and did them perfectly, then, of course, mom and dad would stop yelling, and they would have a happy family.

She tried and tried, week after week, month after month, and year after year. She got straight As. She kept her room spotless. She was always attentive to her mom's moods. And she treated her dad like a king.

And still the fights continued. Nothing she did ever helped very much. Her belief, practiced for many years, was that she could make it all different. That belief helped her feel so much better because it gave her hope.

You see, when she was out in the bushes trying to believe that she was really a princess who had been brought to a bad house, she was very sad. It was a hopeless situation for her if her parents were really out of control. What would happen to her? Who would care for her and love her if they couldn't? It was unthinkable that she was trapped in such a situation. But she *was* trapped, because there really was no wonderful king or queen somewhere who would find their lost daughter and take her to her rightful home.

When she thought about all she could do, she felt hope. If she could just keep her room a little cleaner, if she could just get an A plus instead of an A, if she could do a little better keeping track of her mother's moods, she could make everything okay. It was all in her control. Her family was a good one; she just wasn't doing her part well enough.

So she kept trying and trying and trying, and she kept hoping and hoping and hoping. And then she didn't feel so sad.

There was just one problem with this solution: It never worked. No matter how hard she tried, nothing changed. So, naturally, she figured that she just wasn't good enough. It must be her fault, because if she were just a better girl, theirs would be a happy family.

So this cute and sweet and smart little girl, who was liked by many people, began to think of herself as a failure. She wasn't smart enough, she wasn't nice enough, so she must not be enough of anything.

Slowly, she became convinced that she wasn't a worthwhile person. Life became gray, just drudgery. Nothing much made her sing anymore, but she loved her mom and dad, and felt safe and secure in her fine family. And she lived unhappily ever after.

Poor little Mary. She works so hard. She's a very nice little person, so brave and strong, and she deserves better. She keeps trying and trying, giving her best effort, no matter how often she fails. But instead of feeling good about how brave and strong she is, she feels that she isn't very good at all. Her fantasy keeps her going, and it gives her hope that one day, things will get better if she just tries hard enough. In fact, she keeps trying, right through her entire childhood and into her adult life.

Her hope keeps her going, but it also keeps her feeling like a failure. Because, instead of seeing her courage and resourcefulness, she sees only her inadequacy. She's willing to pay the price of her own self, however, to feel safe in the love of her parents.

Doing the Best We Can

Pam has a fantasy just like Mary's. She believes in it with all her heart. She knows, she just knows, that it is in her power to get her mother to give her the kind of love she has always wanted. *If she can just do it right.*

Kathy has such a fantasy too. Kathy's fantasy is that she comes from a normal and happy family. She, however, is just a negative person, who doesn't know how to appreciate a good thing.

These fantasies work for Pam and Kathy the same way that Mary's worked for her: they protect them from the intolerable pain of their childhoods. Pam's mother didn't love her in the way that Pam needed, and that made Pam's childhood difficult and sad. Kathy's family wasn't really normal, and her father was abusive, especially to Kathy. That made Kathy's childhood frightening and lonely.

Like Mary, Pam and Kathy found a way to avoid that pain. By believing in a different reality, they could believe that they were getting what they needed. These beliefs, false as they actually were, were vital, because they gave both girls the illusion of safety. And safety is crucial in being able to grow up in any healthy way. We all need the security of knowing that our parents will care for us and love us, even if that feeling is a fantasy.

Love and attention are essential for survival through infancy. Without it, babies will fail to grow and develop and will eventually die. (The phenomenon, called *hospitalism*, was first studied by René Spitz at a hospital orphanage in Europe where babies were kept in cribs without any physical contact or affection.)

Research with monkeys that were deprived of their mothers showed that they would attach themselves to an acceptable substitute (which turned out to be a cloth doll instead of a wire doll) and would manage somehow to grow up with this imaginary mother.

Growing babies and children need to be attached and need care and attention in order to develop normally. Just as attaching itself to an imitation mother allows the monkey to feel more mothered and secure, a fantasy of a safe household allows a child to feel safe, secure, and loved, thereby allowing that child to grow.

So, in the face of deprivation, chaos, or abuse, the child begins an effective psychological process that will take her through this part of life. We can look at this process as an adaptation to a difficult situation. When we adapt, we bend, we move, we mold ourselves into a different position or into a different shape in order to relieve pressure or gain some sense of balance or control. Adaptation is a normal and healthy process.

For example, if you are deaf in one ear, you find ways to get people to talk into your good ear. If you can't carry a tune, you decide to learn to play the drums. If your baby sister won't leave your toys alone, you learn to play with them along with her.

Or there can be psychological adaptations. If a spouse refuses to see things your way, you try to understand him better in order to see things his way. If your family has chronic conflicts around the holidays, you decide that you really prefer to spend the holidays with close friends. If you've always wanted a daughter, but only had sons, you think about how nice it will be, when you're older, to have such strong men to help take care of you.

In each of these examples, there is some real loss or deficit, but the person finds a way to work around the problem, to make the situation work as well as it can. This is a sign of psychological strength and health. It shows flexibility. Complaining doesn't make anything any better. Adapting does make things better. It moves things along, it allows progress, growth, and development.

We all have to do this to some degree, depending on the stresses we encounter. And when we make a psychological adaptation, it is usually the best that we can do under the circumstances. We can't do very well without these adaptations. If we couldn't find ways to handle conflict, pain, and disappointment, we would all be in constant turmoil, a mess of raging emotions. In the case of a child who comes from an abusive family, this ability to adapt is not optional—it is necessary for survival.

Our point in all of this is to make clear that psychological defenses are a normal and healthy part of human life. We all have them. Some of them are better than others. For example, trying to excel to please a critical parent will most likely help a person in relationships, school, and employment more than rebelling against everything the parent stands for. Still, each is usually the best that person can do at that time.

The Defense of Denial

"My father didn't beat me, he just lost his temper every now and then."

"My mother wasn't an alcoholic, she just loved martinis."

"It was okay that I had so much responsibility so young, because it really fit my personality."

"Sure, my father hit me, but only when I deserved it."

Do these claims sound familiar? They should, because they are examples of a very common psychological defense, the defense of denial: denial of pain, denial of loss, denial of abuse, *denial of reality*. And it is a very common defense of childhood. Let's look at why that is.

Childhood is a time of natural helplessness. We don't have control of our own lives because we are not capable of exercising it. We are dependent on our caretakers for everything—a home, food and clothing, knowledge about life, safety, and love and nurturing. There's not a lot we can do to make our caregivers provide any of these things any better than they can.

So, if your father can't earn much money, you won't have much. If your mother's not a good cook, you'll eat boring food. If your parents divorce, you'll learn to deal with having two homes. You just can't make parents into something they're not. You are totally at their mercy. You get what they've got to give, and that's it. There is nothing you can do about it. Thankfully, there is usually enough from most parents—certainly enough to get you to adulthood where you can take care of yourself!

But what do you do when you're a child and life is unacceptable? What if there's not just bad food, but *no* food? What if your parents don't just divorce, but your father returns to beat up your mother whenever he gets drunk? One of the best ways to deal with this unacceptable reality is to change it in your own mind, to deny reality, to create your own reality—in effect, to have a fantasy.

The old joke about the pessimist and the optimist at Christmas is a great example of this. The pessimist gets a bicycle. He bemoans his fate: he'll fall down, probably break some bones, miss a lot of school, fail his tests, get left back, and never get into college. He won't ever have much success. The optimist gets a stocking with horse manure in it. "Oh, look," he says excitedly, "Santa left me a pony, but it ran away." Our fantasies create the reality we need.

Let's take an example of how children really do this to protect themselves. Imagine you are a small child with an alcoholic father and a mother who works the swing shift. Your dad starts drinking when he gets home. If it's been a bad day, he may get pretty mad and may spank you really hard for no good reason. He's pretty well out of it by the time your mother leaves for work, yet he's the adult who's supposed to be taking care of you. You're the oldest child of three, you're a girl, and you've started helping around the house because it's obvious that your parents are overwhelmed.

Your dad and mom sort of get along but don't seem to enjoy each other much. Dad keeps drinking, and mom gets depressed. Sometimes, maybe two or three times a month, your dad comes into your room after your mom has left. You're already asleep, but he lies down next to you and starts touching you in strange places. You wake up and smell his bad beer breath on you. You don't move—you just hope he'll go away. Sometimes he does, but sometimes he gets very excited. He puts his hands down your pants and feels you down there. Then, as time goes on, he takes off your pajamas. Pretty soon, he's having sex with you.

He tells you that you are a bad person for doing this, and if you tell anyone, he'll beat you within an inch of your life. You don't say a word. You have reason to believe his threats. You act as though it isn't happening at night, and you never tell anyone about it during the day. You can't imagine anyone can do anything.

What do you do with such a terrible reality? Your father, the person who is supposed to love and support you, beats you and sexually abuses you. He can't care for you at all. Your mother doesn't seem to notice that anything is wrong. You can hardly imagine what she'd do if she found out. Would she blame you as your father does? You are in terrible danger, and you see no way out except to escape into your own private world. You create a different reality for yourself, a fantasy. In this fantasy, your mother and father are really wonderful and caring people. Your mother is basically in control, loving, and thoughtful, though sometimes she loses her patience with you—but only when you've done something to cause her to be upset. She and your father really love each other; they've just been having a hard time lately. Your father doesn't get mad for no good reason, but only for very good reasons. (As in, "Sure, my father hit me, but only when I deserved it.") In this fantasy, you have been singled out for this treatment from your father, including the sexual abuse, because you have been bad in some way, even if you don't know exactly how. So, all in all, as the fantasy works itself out, you are a basically bad child being raised by basically good parents.

It Is Better to Be a Bad Child in a Safe World, Than a Good Child in a Dangerous World.

We hope that we have begun to show how much safer it is for a child to believe this fantasy than to believe in reality. Reality is terrifying, perhaps life-threatening, surely soul-threatening. This fantasy is safe, secure, hopeful. It is less dangerous to be a bad child in a safe world than to be a good child in a dangerous world. The fantasy of loving parents helps you grow and survive till you are on your own and do have control.

Some theorists consider the need for mastery to be one of the basic forces pushing us as individuals. By mastery, we mean the ability to master more and more tasks and situations in life. So, early in life, we feel good when we can walk, talk, eat with a spoon, tie our shoes, and ride a two-wheeler. Then the tasks we want to master become more complicated. We may want to learn to play an instrument, get an A on an exam, win at tennis, sink a basketball, get a job, head the student council. But a theme in the push to gain mastery is the need for control. Rather than to feel helpless, which is always a risky situation, we want to feel as though we can act effectively for ourselves; we want to feel that we have control.

Also, a concept called *learned helplessness* can play an important role in a child's development. According to this theory, a person may *learn* that there is nothing she can do about something in her life. If she truly believes that she is helpless, she will give up; she will become passive and hopeless and eventually depressed. But if this person can have a fantasy of being powerful, then that fantasy will protect her from hopelessness and despair. In her fantasy, she thinks she knows what she can do and what will work. This sense of predictability *feels* like control.

The need for control certainly varies from person to person. Some trust that things will work out without their input. Others become anxious if they don't feel they can influence everything around them. But the ability to have some control is important. Since there is not a lot a small child can control, she is vulnerable to what everyone else does. Still, the need is there to feel in control of whatever she can.

In an abusive or deprived home, the child has little real control. She is at the whim of her parents. If they are out of control, it is even scarier for her. Her whole sense of safety in the world is gone. She must find a way to get it back.

So the motivation for childhood fantasy that denies an intolerable reality is the most seductive motivation there can be: it is about survival. The child cannot sustain herself in the reality as it is; her denial of reality protects her. But, as with many desperate or extreme measures, the cost is very high. Its high cost does not mean that the strategy is a bad one, only that it has a very high price.

In fact, the price is the ultimate—it is the self, which the child will sacrifice in the service of the life-sustaining fantasy. In other words, by blaming herself for the bad things that happen to her in order to feel safe, she discounts feelings, perceptions, events, her own competence and ability. That is, she denies anything that interferes with her fantasy.

So the body survives. The child goes to school, has friends, maybe goes on to college, and gets married. But she has lost, at least for the time being, huge parts of herself. If she must deny reality as she grows up, she must deny learning about herself. If she has changed her sense of herself from that of a good girl in a bad world into that of a bad girl in a good world, she has damaged and distorted her sense of herself in order to survive.

Let's go back to Pam to see how this necessary protection will ultimately lead to trouble. Pam's story is less dramatic than the scenario we have just described, but may be more common. The external circumstances are less extreme, but the consequences of denial and fantasy are the same.

Pam's situation is *more subtle*, but it is very poignant. As you recall, she was a smart and lively child, eager to please and to be loved. Unfortunately for her, her siblings came so quickly, three boys in a row, that by the time she was six, there were three younger children, all needing more care than she (because they were younger), and all treated as more important (because they were boys).

Here is this little girl, getting left in the dust at only two. There was no time for anyone to admire or delight in her. She was expected to pick up her toys, not spill her milk, and not pick on her little brother. At four, no one got excited about how quickly she was able to learn. They just wanted her to keep her voice down. And at six, she got criticism and an assignment of chores when she got home after having spent all day at school, a time when she needed to be reconnected with her parents.

She was just a little girl, but she was expected to be big and to help, and even to support her mother. There was no time for her to be scared or needy. She just got pushed along. It wouldn't have been surprising if she had just stopped expecting anything special, and had simply done what was expected and toed the line. It's easy to imagine a quiet, withdrawn, and pretty hopeless little person, learning to be satisfied with a few morsels.

But Pam was a fighter. She fought for what she wanted instead of giving in to the pressures around her. She didn't believe that there was nothing for her (that awareness would have been emotionally devastating). No, Pam believed that she could get what she needed if she could only figure out how. Her lack of compliance made her a difficult child for her mother to deal with. Her mother got angry often. She blamed Pam for causing trouble and, as Pam got older, even threatened to send her to a boarding school for wayward girls.

So, Pam's fantasy was that there was enough love for her if she could just figure out how to be lovable. Since she never got the love, she concluded that she wasn't lovable. Coupled with the constant criticism she received, this belief in her unlovability grew strong, supported by her mother's comments about how bad she was. But love is important, and Pam wouldn't give up trying to be what her mother wanted so that she could be loved.

Her fantasy required that she be a bad child (unlovable, rebellious, troublesome, difficult) in a good world (a mother who could love her). For Pam growing up, this was preferable to the reality of her being a good child (lovable, just as she was) in a depriving and hostile world (her mother had little love to give and was constantly critical).

The equation is clear: if Pam has a loving mother, but she can't get that mother to love her, she must not be lovable, and she must come to think of herself as unlovable.

Pam had enormous strengths that enabled her to fight for herself. And because she didn't become a passive victim of poor upbringing, she went on in life to do productive things—to study, to learn, and to contribute. But happiness was beyond her grasp.

She has had to pay the price for her fantasy now, during adulthood, because that fantasy was so vital during childhood. The fantasy created the illusion of safety by assuming that her mother was good (and that she was bad). But how can a person ultimately have a positive self-concept and an optimistic view of life if she believes that she is basically a bad or unlovable person who deserves the bad things that happen to her? She has distorted herself in order to preserve the reality she needed and she feels that distortion every day.

Pam thinks of herself as basically unlovable. Yet, since feeling loved is such a basic need, she doesn't give up on getting it.

She struggles in all of her relationships to get that feeling of being loved. But since she doesn't feel that she will get it naturally, she works extra hard to try to make herself lovable. Unfortunately, even when people do care deeply for her, she never feels it because she doesn't believe it. Loneliness and disconnection are major feelings in her life. Since they are the result of the childhood fantasy that she carries with her, they are constant, and they are unaffected by current reality.

Pam is critical of herself because of her belief in her basic defectiveness; no matter what she succeeds in, she discounts her accomplishments. She is unable, therefore, to build her self-esteem. In general, Pam feels depressed. She has a lot of self-hatred: she criticizes herself constantly, she cuts herself down every time she does something good, and she breaks off connections with people because she does not expect good things to come out of those relationships and doesn't want to hang around for the inevitable disappointment.

All of this happens to Pam because of what she did as a child to protect herself. The psychological defense that worked so well in childhood becomes the source of psychological pain in adulthood. The symptoms of chronic depression, hopelessness, and self-hatred become intolerable and are what bring Pam to seek therapy.

Let's look at another example of this. The symptoms that Kathy developed from maintaining her fantasy were more acute and dramatic than Pam's, though the basic mechanism was the same.

It is devastating when a child's caretaker becomes her abuser. That caretaker, the child assumes, is there to help her. If the child is good, she will be treated well, but if she is bad, then she will be punished. That would be normal.

So, in order for Kathy to tolerate her father's abuse, she had to believe she was bad enough to deserve it. Her family's blaming her for being so sad all the time (though her sadness was clearly a normal response to what was happening to her) added to her feeling of defectiveness. She was isolated from her whole family, left alone to make sense of the world. The only thing that made sense was her basic badness.

This sense about herself colored everything that happened to her. Though she was bright and creative, she didn't think of herself as such, or as successful at anything. And since she thought of herself as such a bad person, she could never really accept the love of her husband and children. Eventually, her sense of being entirely useless led to suicidal impulses. What had once been a life-saving psychological defense was about to destroy her.

Good Pain/Bad Pain

The defenses that worked so well in childhood became the source of the psychological pain in adulthood that led both Pam and Kathy to therapy. What they did to keep themselves safe, and what they automatically keep doing to themselves, is now hurting them.

Let us explain why we call this "bad pain." Someone like Kathy, for example, comes to therapy in a suicidal state because she feels like a bad and useless person. But she doesn't feel that way because it's true that she's actually bad. She feels that way because it was a defense she had to develop in order to survive. Now, it's *all* she feels about herself. So we call it "bad" because it has become what she believes about herself, what she doesn't like about herself, and what she suffers with constantly.

When Kathy starts therapy, all she can talk about is how bad she is, what horrible self-esteem she has, how no one could possibly love her, and on and on. Nothing the therapist says can help her feel better, because she believes these things deep in her heart. Week after week, she continues to talk about these bad feelings, because they are the only ones she knows.

Yet these feelings are only there to support her fantasies. They aren't about anything real—that is, her self-criticisms are inaccurate. The content of her complaints is, basically, false. Therefore, it doesn't matter how much she talks about her bad feelings, or thinks about them, or works on them, they can never change as long as she still believes her fantasy. She begins to feel that nothing will help, and this only adds to her feeling of hopelessness.

So we call these feelings "bad pain" because working on them in therapy doesn't make anything any better. This kind of pain is not the natural pain that comes from the struggle for growth and change; it is the pain of defense, of maintaining the status quo. This is the pain of stagnation, helplessness, and hopelessness. *It doesn't matter how much you feel it, it never gets any better.*

There is another kind of pain, though, that we call "good pain." Although it may seem like a contradiction to call any pain "good," we think this is a very important distinction to make. Good pain is the pain we feel when we change. By definition, we cannot both change and have things stay the same; good pain, therefore, is the pain of loss and mourning.

We also call it good pain because it accomplishes something—it is a part of the normal grieving process. We all have a natural ability to grieve a loss. Of course we feel many awful feelings when we grieve—anger, sadness, isolation, confusion, and fear. But as, in the grip of these feelings, we experience our loss (as long as nothing interferes), there is progress. The feelings change, some get better, some get worse for a while as new wounds open, new ideas develop, and our life shifts to accommodate the loss.

Eventually, we are able to go on, even if there is always true sadness over what we have lost. But if we have done our grieving, we are not likely to continue to experience overwhelming sadness. The sadness is real, but it is just a feeling. It is not crippling or destructive to the self. Good pain is the pain of grief, of progress, of growth and change.

For Pam and Kathy, feeling better will involve exchanging one pain for another, exchanging bad pain for good pain. They will have to give up the pain of self-blame in exchange for the pain of grief. Pam will have to grieve the loss of her mother's love, which she never really had, nor will ever have. Kathy will have to grieve the loss of her family, who never took good care of her or treated her well.

Pam and Kathy (as is the case with most of us) are afraid to exchange one pain for the other. They have developed defenses that protect them from the pain of childhood trauma. Even as adults, they believe they cannot tolerate that pain. They hold on to the old pain, the bad pain, as if for dear life, fighting the good pain.

We bring this natural resistance to change to therapy. It comes from the defense of denial, a powerful and protective force of childhood. But, like many defenses, it eventually outlives its usefulness and becomes a negative force in life. The cost of the defense is enormous—self-hatred and self-blame, and all of the destructiveness these feelings cause in life.

If we are going to change, we have to learn to fight that natural resistance; we have to confront our denial. By giving up the fantasy and the denial, and by learning to face reality, with its real pain, therapy can work. But we have to exchange one pain for the other.

It should be clear now that denying the reality of the past and fearing to face its pain prevent movement and change. But clinging to the hope that someone's love will be all that we need to feel better is another obstacle to change, especially for women. In the next chapter as we look at the relationship trap, we explore what happens to women as they get hooked by the hope that the next relationship is going to make all the difference.

— 4 —

The Relationship Trap:
Hazards for Women
in the Therapy Relationship

Girls are nice, like sugar and spice or so goes the old rhyme. Familiar sayings like this, as harmless as they may seem, do express cultural realities. Perhaps we don't pay much attention to them because we're so used to them or because we think of them as just harmless old sayings. But what does it mean for us women, and what does it cost us, to be expected to want little for ourselves except the happiness of helping others?

All throughout life, the expectations are the same: we are to be pleasing and pretty, and to make those around us feel good. As adults, we associate the mothering role with women and unconsciously expect women to nurture and take care of us. So, when women are aggressive or challenging, we are often hurt and disappointed. That's not the way it's supposed to be.

A little girl, dressed in a white pinafore, neat, clean, and well-behaved may be a stereotype that we feel we have moved beyond. And yet a grown woman executive is expected to "dress up" for success. She must be feminine, but not too sexy. She must be competent, but not aggressive. She must lead and show her authority without making anyone uncomfortable. If she cannot strike this delicate balance, she is sure to be criticized. If her male colleague is forceful, he is considered to be a real leader; if she acts the same, she is labeled a "bitch." It's quite a challenge to do it right. Most of the time, it's impossible.

What begins as a cultural role, imposed from the outside, is eventually internalized. One of the most important lessons we learn is that we are responsible for and valued for the success of our relationships. Another lesson we learn is that we are not expected to achieve too much or to draw too much attention to ourselves. From the classroom to the boardroom, a woman learns that she will not be called on, and that if she speaks up too much, she will be resented.

A classic psychological study by Matina Horner illustrates young women's fear of excelling and standing out. In this study, college women and men were asked to tell a story based on a single sentence. The men's sentence was, "At the end of the first semester in medical school, John found himself at the top of his class." For the women, the sentence was the same, except that the subject of the sentence was Jane.

The outcome of this study is troubling. The men's stories typically portrayed John as becoming a huge success: having a busy practice, becoming president of the medical society, and, in general, being held in high esteem. The women's stories were shockingly different. Jane was looked down on and ostracized by her peers, had an unhappy life, and, in some stories, was even beaten and mutilated.

The message from this is that it can feel literally life-threatening for girls to focus on themselves, to attract too much attention, to work for themselves. We are afraid that we will be hated if we achieve success or recognition. But if we hide ourselves, we will be loved. If we work for ourselves, we will be isolated. Better, then, to have love than success.

Our Job Is Our Relationships

These messages are clear and steady during our formative years, and we learn them well. We learn that our job is doing relationships, and that our value is our success in making them work. (In fact, we often take complete responsibility for them.) We are not trained to think of ourselves as autonomous individuals, expressing ourselves in the world according to our own values, skills, or beliefs. Instead we get the message that we must find the most important relationship of all—the right relationship with a man—through which to express ourselves. Our value will then be his value, our success will be his. The classic role for a woman, still very much alive today, is to help a man in his life, support him in his endeavors, and raise his family. The bargain we make is that in exchange for giving ourselves over to him, we will be taken care of. Of course, many women have found other options and satisfying life paths. Yet these other paths are often seen as exceptions to the more "natural" nurturing role. It is difficult to erase the cultural imprint from ourselves. (Colette Dowling's book *The Cinderella Complex*, though published in 1981, still resonates as a classic description of this life pattern for women.)

Even in today's world, with so many more options available to young women, the expectation is getting through loud and clear—we must tend to all of our relationships from the very beginning of our lives.

One of us, Joan, remembers this from the first day of school. Of course, we were all scared. Dressed in our first-day-of-school finest, we waited on the playground on that crisp fall day to go inside our school for the first time. The teachers came out to tell us where each of us would go. There were two classrooms, the regular kindergarten room, and an extra one, because there were too many children for just one room (the beginning of the baby boom). Since I have a twin brother, we two would go to different rooms. But as it happened, my two little girlfriends from our block, as well as my brother all went to the big classroom, and I went alone to the other room. I felt left out, sad, scared, and lonely, but I was managing.

One little girl was having an especially difficult time. She couldn't stop crying. For some reason, the teacher approached me and made me her buddy. Would I stay with her, I was asked, and help her? "Help her what?" I remember wondering to myself. But I don't think I said anything. I just did my best, I did what I was told. On my first lonely, scary day of school, my job was to help someone else! I figured that I wasn't supposed to think about me.

All little girls learn this lesson in one way or another. And though the lessons are clear by kindergarten, they begin before that. It is usually early in the relationship with her mother that a little girl first learns how to care for another.

There is something special about the relationship between a mother and her girl child that leads to a unique kind of emotional give and take. Under ideal circumstances, this teaches the girl how to care about others and how to let them care about her. But, more often, it teaches the girl to ignore her own feelings and think of others' feelings instead. Luise Eichenbaum and Susie Orbach have written brilliantly about this in their book *Understanding Women.*

This is how it happens: A mother has a girl. She sees another female in this little girl, and a female is, traditionally, one who gives care and nurturing. So, unconsciously, the mother expects some of this kind of nurturing from her little daughter. And she is pleased when her daughter cares for her.

But to complicate this picture, the mother has already learned that she is a devalued and unappreciated member of society. She has been learning to think of others instead of herself *her* whole life, so she is chronically deprived of nurturing. She sees in this little bundle of love someone who might provide some of this caring for her. When the little girl responds to her needs, the mother is gratified and rewards this behavior. The girl learns that she can make mother happy by making her feel good. And a happy mother is a better mother. The girl learns very early that the best way for her to be cared for is to care first for another.

In a healthy relationship, the mother has gotten enough of her own emotional needs met that she doesn't expect or need the girl to meet hers. Instead there is a give and take, a reciprocity. The girl learns that relationships have a give and take. She learns about herself in this relationship and thinks about herself as someone who is always "in relationship."

The researchers at the Stone Center at Wellesley, including Jean Baker Miller, Irene Stiver, Judith Jordan, and others, write about this "relational self" as a healthy ideal in which girls learn about themselves through their relationships. Carol Gilligan, in her book, *In a Different Voice*, writes about the "self-in-relation" as a relational style of females that is different from that of males, though a positive one because it encourages a healthy concern for others.

These are the ideal circumstances. (And, fortunately, this relational style of women is gaining more value in our culture). But if the mother, as is often the case, has been deprived herself, she doesn't have enough to give the daughter. So the daughter begins to give to others (beginning with mother) before she has received enough herself. Of course, she is then likely to grow up to be a deprived mother, and if she doesn't do something to change, she will begin the cycle all over again.

Even if the mother is unhappy because of things that have nothing to do with the daughter, the daughter may have difficulty recognizing this. She takes on the responsibility for her mother's feelings and works to make her happy. Often in adulthood, women continue this tendency and may get lost in the focus on another person. A woman will then end up defining herself by the other person's feelings instead of by her own.

Pam has fallen into this trap. Her mother, herself raised by a strict mother who offered her little love, did not learn how to give love easily. Her children were all destined to suffer as a result. Pam, her only daughter, came to be viewed by her as a source of support and as a helper.

Pam is a perfect example of a little girl focusing on her mother's needs in hopes of getting a little something for herself. Overwhelmed quickly by a rapid succession of births, Pam's mother didn't have a chance to learn to care emotionally for her children. Of course, she did her best.

But one of the ways she coped was to expect more of her daughter than of her sons, to expect her daughter to care, to understand, to help.

Too needy herself, she was oblivious to the reality that Pam was just a very little girl, incapable of understanding others' feelings or of meeting their needs. But since Pam's mother needed and expected this of Pam, she was constantly disappointed in her. She came to see Pam as selfish and difficult, although Pam was just a normal child. But, of course, any normal child is trouble. Pam's mother took Pam's natural behavior personally, as though Pam weren't trying hard enough to be helpful or good.

A lifetime of conflict was established. Pam's mother wanted more of her daughter than she could possibly deliver. Pam tried to please her mother, but never could. Her mother was chronically disappointed and angry, so Pam tried harder. But she was only a child and couldn't meet her mother's needs, unfulfilled because of a lifetime of deprivation, so she failed. Her mother grew more angry and critical, and Pam became increasingly hurt and defensive. She reacted, got punished, then tried harder. Pam's mother thought she was just trouble, and Pam thought her mother didn't love her.

Her mother's behavior, we can see, has nothing to do with Pam herself, but Pam has never known this. She has always considered herself responsible for her mother's lack of love and affection for her. This is her fantasy: that she could actually do something about her mother's behavior. Since her mother never changed, Pam assumed that she was doing something wrong. For Pam, her girlhood sense of responsibility for relationships, coupled with any child's natural tendency to create a fantasy of loving parents, leaves her ultimately feeling like a failure in her relationship with her mother and, by extension, a failure in all of her relationships.

From this relationship with her mother, Pam learned that it was important, desperately important, to meet other peoples' needs in order to win their care and love. She also knew that her efforts would not succeed and that no matter how hard she tried, she would never get the love she so desperately needed. She learned to value her performance in relationships above all else. In a sense, the entire responsibility for the relationship rested on her shoulders. It was all up to her. (We are reminded of a line from Rosanne Barr: "How do I know I'm a woman? Because I'm responsible for everything, and everything's my fault!")

Is it any surprise that Pam would bring her relational style into her therapy? Ostensibly, she goes into therapy to get help, but therapy is itself a relationship. The only way Pam knows how to get anything out of a relationship is to work like crazy to get the person to love her. Here she is, seeking help from another person to help her feel better. How can she possibly avoid feeling that she has to work to make that person care about her, and that only if she works hard enough at it will she get any of the care that she needs? She can't avoid it. Neither can she avoid, even in the therapy relationship, the fear that she will never be good enough. She must always try her hardest to be lovable. At the same time, she carries with her the discouraging belief that, no matter what she does, she will never succeed in winning love from another. Her therapy begins to focus on her need to establish this care and love with her therapist.

Kathy, too, was obsessed with her impact on others, and was terrified that she would ruin any relationship; she would become paralyzed with fear when anything went wrong for anyone she was involved with. Obviously, one cannot control all the unpredictable things that happen in life, but Kathy acted as if she should be able to so that her family would never be unhappy.

This attitude took her to extremes. One beautiful Saturday, early in the spring, she and her husband were deciding what to do with their two children. They might go to the Children's Museum. But, since it was the first really beautiful day of the year, Kathy thought they should go for a picnic. Everything seemed to be going well. But a storm suddenly came up, and they had to pile quickly into the car and drive home. Kathy blamed herself for ruining everyone's day. If they had just gone to the museum, everything would have been okay; she should have kept her mouth shut.

Kathy really preferred the picnic idea. As a full-time mother, she had had her fill of the museums that winter and wanted a chance to be outside with her husband and kids. She expressed her preference, and, bam! Look what happened! Everything was ruined. This is how she saw life—that if she wasn't totally self-less, she would suffer in the end. Over and over again, she rein-forced her belief that it was wrong to think of herself ahead of those she loved.

Is it any wonder that Kathy tried, as often as she could, to stay cut off from her own desires, and to please others without thinking of herself? This is clearly an adaptive solution, since she was bound to feel some sort of punishment when she thought of herself at all. Concentrating on her own needs would usually bring an increase in shame and self-hatred, and a heightening of all of her symptoms—drinking, bingeing and purging, insom-nia, and depression.

What could she possibly do to help herself in a therapy rela-tionship? She was a bad wife and a bad mother, and in her mind, she should fix those those things first before she tackled her own problems. In therapy, she focused, then, on what a bad wife she was to her husband and what a bad mother she was to her children. She thought about how these important people in her life saw her and tried to avoid looking at her own sadness and confusion.

Looking into her past, the reasons for this pattern are clear. The fantasy that had helped her through her abusive childhood was that she'd only gotten what she deserved. In this fantasy, her parents were basically good people who would have been kind and loving to any child who deserved it. Since she was treated so poorly, she concluded, she must not deserve love and kind-ness; she must simply be bad. She imagined that all a therapist could do for her was to help her learn to tolerate being this bad.

A tiny bit of comfort about being such a bad person was all she could hope for.

In her family, Kathy helped maintain a fragile balance by accepting the role of the bad member. For her, taking care of relationships didn't mean making those relationships pleasant; it simply meant learning to accept being the bad one within the relationship.

Taking care of relationships may take on many different forms, and most of those get played out in the therapy relationship. Given her belief about relationships, Kathy had to believe that her therapist, like her family, thought of her as the "bad one." In psychological terms, she "projected" her beliefs onto her therapist. She put her therapist in the role of the one who thought of her as bad and then related to her therapist as that person.

This kind of projection is something we all do in all kinds of relationships, but because of all the importance and hope the client places in the relationship with her therapist, the projection is profound. The therapist has to work mightily to be seen as anything but the person the client has imagined her to be. In order to gain awareness and control over what she is doing, the client must do some serious exploration of her past. There she will find the real relationship from her past that she is playing out in her present. Coming to terms with the past is essential to seeing reality in the present.

How Do You Want Me to Be?

Because women can't avoid the sense of responsibility for relationships, we bring that compulsion with us into therapy. It's as if we have to get the therapy relationship all tuned up and in good shape before we can try to get a little bit out of it. Why we came to therapy can become almost an afterthought, as we turn our efforts toward making the relationship okay.

Elaine is a good example of someone who focuses on the therapeutic relationship so exclusively that her needs become entirely irrelevant. She was seeing a highly regarded therapist for chronic depression. She liked her therapist and recognized that he was trying to help her. But after more than a year, she didn't feel significantly better. She wondered if the therapy was going the way it should, and she even wondered if this therapist knew how to help her. Bright and well-educated, she could have asked some questions to find out if she and her therapist were headed in the right direction. But if she asked these questions, he would know that she was dissatisfied. And *she didn't want to hurt his feelings.*

Like most women, Elaine is skilled at thinking about what might make someone else feel good. (However, she never asked her former therapist what would have made *him* feel good. Helping her get well would have made him happy, even if it meant finding someone new to help her. But Elaine couldn't be that explicit and confrontational with her therapist; she had to work on this problem on her own.) Elaine figured that her therapist would feel satisfied if she should progress; so she began to present herself as getting well. Pretty soon, she had the therapist convinced, and they concluded the therapy.

Elaine left, relieved to be out of the predicament. Still, she's not any better. She just hasn't hurt anyone's feelings (except her own). She's free to try someone else without making the first therapist look bad. Although she didn't get better, she did preserve (in her mind) the relationship.

Being the way we think the therapist wants us to be is a classic stance for women in any relationship. In therapy, we want to fulfill the role of the good patient by doing and saying what we think the therapist wants us to do and say. Patients of Freudian therapists report erotic dreams about their therapists. Patients in Jungian therapy dream in archetypes. ("I want whatever he wants," a typical stance for a traditional married woman, is not an act—it is what the woman really *feels.*)

We women have spent our entire lives training to be the good helper and partner. Our behavior is automatic. It is also invisible because it is simply what everyone expects of us. Why should it be any different with a therapist? After all, everyone wants to feel good in her relationships, and a therapist feels good when the patient is doing well. Thus an invisible and secret collusion begins.

This is especially true when the therapist is a man. Men, after all, have also been socialized to have their own expectations of women. Just as women have been taught that their role is to cater to men, men have learned to expect to be catered to by women. And just as women's attention to others is unconscious and automatic, so is men's expectation of certain kinds of care from women.

A classic dynamic between men and women is one in which the woman feels the man's feelings for him, thus protecting him from them. It makes a certain kind of sense. Women learn to pay attention to feelings. (We're not saying that they're necessarily better at dealing with those feelings, or we probably wouldn't be writing this book. But they are allowed to have them, and are sometimes devalued because they have too many of them!) Men learn to ignore their feelings. They're not supposed to have them; after all, big boys don't cry. So it is inevitable that women will play the role of the carriers of emotion.

The most enlightened man may still have within him, though unconsciously, a sense that things are as they should be when his emotions are tended to by a woman. A female patient acting pleasingly for a male therapist may not set off any alarms. After all, this is the ways things are supposed to be.

One might think that therapists, through years of training, would be be alert to these dynamics. As therapists, our goal is to promote mental health in all of our patients, male or female. Toward that end, we wouldn't want our patients taking care of our emotional needs; rather, we would be trying to keep them. But we are people, too, most of us raised in this culture, and share unconscious beliefs about the gender roles and appropriate behaviors of men and women. This is equally true for both men and women, and for both therapists and clients.

In a classic study by Broverman et al., therapists were asked to describe what they considered to be a psychologically healthy male, female, and person (gender neutral) using a checklist of opposite characteristics. Some of the characteristics included were passive or assertive, brave or timid, talkative or quiet, and even good or bad at math and science. The startling result of this study was that although the characteristics of a healthy male were judged to be the same as those of a healthy person, the characteristics of a healthy female were judged to be the same as those of an *unhealthy* one.

For example, while healthy males (and healthy "people") were considered to be assertive, courageous, independent, and self-confident, healthy females were considered to be passive, fearful, dependent, and to have low self-esteem. Apparently, unhealthy behaviors are considered normal in women—even by therapists. Clearly, our gender role expectations transcend even professional training.

So, if everyone's expectations of women are that they be relatively passive, dependent, and helpful, what happens to a woman in therapy? Often for her, the point of her therapy becomes pleasing the therapist. Her goal then, has less to do with personal change or growth than with maintaining the status quo, and fulfilling her cultural role. Don't forget, it's better to be loved than to be successful. The need is very strong to be what we expect ourselves to be. Our sense of self depends on it. Our sense of self depends on how we are in our relationships.

How Did a Relationship Become Such a Bad Thing?

Now that we have described so many hazards in relationships for women, let us backtrack a little. Our intention is certainly not to say that relationships are bad; they are necessary and important. And women's focus on care for others and on maintaining relationships is valuable to all of us. It is important for children and for families, and it is a crucial characteristic missing from many of our male-dominated institutions. Relationships are vital to healthy human living.

And there is nothing wrong with having a relationship with your therapist. We are social creatures, after all, and we learn about who we are and how we affect the world through our relationships. When things go relatively well, we get a clear image of who we are and positive self-esteem from those we deal with socially and professionally. When things go wrong, particularly in our early years, we can get a distorted picture of reality and of ourselves. So it is often what we learn about ourselves in those early relationships that needs to be unlearned in therapy.

In addition to serving the purpose of fulfilling our cultural roles, many of the problematic ways we learn to be in relationships are part of the adaptive fantasy that we developed as children. Kathy, for example, had a fantasy that she was the bad one in the family, and it helped her believe that she had loving parents. She creates that same fantasy with her therapist. The therapist, then, becomes the "good" one, and Kathy remains the "bad" one. Her mission becomes simply to be tolerated for being bad.

As long as Kathy focuses on this aspect of the relationship, she will move nowhere because the fantasy simply maintains the status quo. The fantasy helped Kathy survive when she was little, and she believes (unconsciously, without putting it into words) that it helps her survive today. Unfortunately, it does little else, because it keeps her stuck right where she is and prevents the therapy relationship from helping her to grow.

But if the therapy relationship is a good one, Kathy can safely challenge the status quo. She can dare to believe that she is not bad. Her therapist is not the good one, in a position to judge her badness. If she does not continually see herself as bad in the relationship, she can begin to unravel the fantasy that she was bad. Once she can accept the fantasy for what it is, she has the potential to see the truth and, from there, to deal with the real pain in her life. The safety of the relationship makes her work and change possible.

So the therapy relationship is a necessary tool for accomplishing this kind of change—so long as it *is* a tool for change, not an end in itself. The relationship *itself* doesn't produce growth; you don't get better simply by being in the relation-ship—it is the work that you do *within* the relationship that is the source of change.

Women especially are at risk to see the therapy relationship as an end in itself. Here is the paradox: while it's not safe for women to think about themselves, in therapy, they are supposed to. The people around them are used to being made to feel bet-ter. So if a woman is good at this style of relating, no one notices anything. This is how a woman is supposed to be good, and it is how a good woman is supposed to be. So women in therapy may keep working harder and harder at what is supposed to help, and they may be so skilled at this style of relating that the ther-apist is not even aware that something is missing.

The original reasons for seeking therapy, the original goals, then get lost in the responsibility for monitoring the relation-ship. If a woman in therapy can stop focusing on being good at all costs, she can use the relationship to work on some real goals that can be accomplished in therapy.

How will you know whether your therapy is likely to be pro-ductive or not? How can you tell whether you're doing some real work or are stuck doing the same old thing? The next chapter will show you what it looks like if you've gotten yourself stuck.

— 5 —

Five Warning Signs
That You're Wasting
Your Time

"He's a really wonderful guy, sensitive, and very insightful," confided Sharon as she lunched with Kate. "It feels so wonderful when he understands me and cares about me. I feel like I've been waiting for this all of my life."

"So, this is a good thing," Kate responded, wanting her close friend to feel her empathy and understanding.

A little encouragement was all that Sharon needed, and she was eager to elaborate. "I hope that maybe I really can be loved this time. I think about him a lot during the day."

Kate was glad that her friend finally felt good about something. Sharon had been depressed for the better part of a year, and Kate had been concerned about her. Maybe she was finally going to pull out of it. Still, to Kate, something here didn't feel quite right.

She thought about what she should say while the waiter brought their iced teas. As they swirled sweetener into their drinks, she tentatively asked, "Do you feel a little bit preoccupied by this relationship?"

"Yes, yes, I do," sighed Sharon. "But I think it's okay, because this one is good for me."

"But the man is unavailable." Kate said. "I mean, I want you to be happy. I don't want to put a damper on things for you. But I'm not sure how he's different than some of the other men you've cared for: perfect, except that you can't have him."

"I know. I know it sounds the same. But this is different. It's true I can't have him. But it doesn't matter. He's still the most important man in my life."

"Yes, I hear that he is," Kate said, gently. "But, you know, if someone were overhearing us, they'd think you were talking about your boyfriend and not about your therapist. Does that bother you a little bit?"

"Oh, I know it sounds that way. But I'm not worried because I know that Len has my best interests at heart. Besides, I'm sure I'll get past this pretty soon. It feels so good for now. I just hope Len never figures out how I'm feeling. I'd be so embarrassed. Meanwhile, I'll dream on."

A dream is all that Sharon may get—a dream that this relationship, by virtue of how good it feels, will make her better. If all she can focus on is her fantasy, she will not be able to deal with the reality of her life. Yes, a positive relationship is a crucial part of a successful therapy. But what you *do* with that relationship is more important.

Enjoying Therapy

Sharon thinks that her positive feelings mean that her therapy is going to work. In fact, they more likely mean that her therapy is getting stuck. The first warning sign that a therapy is stuck is that it feels much too good. Sharon isn't planning to use the feelings she has for Len (which are, largely, transference) to help her understand herself and her problems better. She's just enjoying them, fantasizing about what can happen between her and Len, and she doesn't want any interference with her pleasure. How much is she willing to pay for this? Because it's going to cost her: in time, in money, and in lost opportunities for growth and change.

Enjoying therapy too much is an important indicator that a therapy is about to go off track. The kind of enjoyment we are talking about is the kind that Sharon is experiencing. She is steeping herself in her pleasure in this relationship, and is unwilling to look at what that pleasure means. Just being with Len makes her feel good, and from that she concludes that just being with Len will make her better in all aspects of her life.

Therapy doesn't have to feel bad in order to work, although if there's no pain or struggle, it's not likely that much is being accomplished. And it's fine to feel good about a therapist, even to think about him or her at different times, or to use the therapist as a reference point, a mentor, or a guide. But what makes Sharon's preoccupation, Sharon's kind of pleasure, a warning sign that she is enjoying therapy too much?

When therapy is the high point of your week, there's a problem. Therapy is supposed to *enhance* your life, it's not supposed to *be* your life. It's a problem if you think about your therapist all of the time and want to be with him all of the time. It's a problem if your goal is to be appealing, and you try to amuse or entertain your therapist so that he will think more highly of you.

Therapy is supposed to be hard work. You may look forward to it and appreciate it, but if it is too pleasurable, you may be enjoying the relationship itself, as Sharon does, instead of paying attention to whether or not the therapy relationship is helping you make the changes you want to make.

A positive feeling about your therapist is an important aspect of therapy, but it shouldn't be the predominant theme. The relationship is there to help you work on your problems, look at things that you keep hidden, face difficult issues, and really get through them. This wonderful relationship is there to help you, not to be an end in itself. If it is, you may be working to get your therapist to like you, and then waiting and hoping for *that* to change your life.

Therapy Is a 10, but Life a 2

There are other signs that Sharon's therapy is in trouble. One of them is that, as happy as Sharon is about her therapy, her life is a mess. When she went in to therapy, for example, she complained that her financial situation was unstable. She wasn't budgeting her money or planning for the future, and when she needed something in an emergency, she often had to borrow from friends. That problem hasn't gotten any better—in fact it seems worse. When she fantasizes about Len, she imagines herself looking incredibly chic. She has been spending more money on clothes because she wants to be appealing to him. Buying clothes with Len in mind, however, is hardly improving her life. If she were talking about it in therapy, it might be helpful because she could understand what her spending problem was about and learn to control it. But as long as Sharon is trying to impress Len, she isn't going to tell him things that embarrass her.

In addition, Sharon had been thinking about getting some more advanced training so that she could either seek a promotion at work or look for a better position. But she has lost interest in this; her energy is too focused on Len. She's losing ground where she had hoped to gain.

In Sharon's case, as things now stand, therapy is a 10, but life is a 2. She clearly is not progressing toward any of her original goals. Her therapy feels good, but her life hasn't shown any improvement.

It is much healthier for the patient when therapy is a 2, and life a 10. Therapy often feels bad, because you are dealing with difficult or painful issues. But dealing with these issues should make your life better. Therapy shouldn't be an end in itself, but a tool to help your real life and your real relationships.

Feeling Stuck

Sharon hasn't yet experienced the feeling that her therapy has gotten stuck—a common problem for many people, often those who have been in therapy much longer than she has. You know that you want to achieve something, you go to therapy to get it, you seem to be reaching for your goal, but you are making little or no progress. You talk about the same issues over and over again, and yet they never seem to change.

There are several reasons why the therapy can get stuck. Often, despite the most honest of intentions, you may not be perfectly honest with your therapist. Deep inside, you know about something that is very painful, frightening, or shameful. On some level, you know this is a problem, and you want it to go away. But you don't want to feel as bad as you fear you will if you deal with it, so you avoid it in therapy.

Something that you are avoiding that strongly is likely to be very important and is probably interfering with your life. Avoiding it in therapy will definitely interfere with achieving your goals. So you may be stuck because, in a way, you are choosing to be stuck: you are keeping your pain submerged, despite your desire to expose and relinquish it.

Of course, you might be stuck because your therapist does not know how to help you beyond your present stage. This can be painful and difficult for any patient to accept. We don't want to believe that this person whom we trust and depend upon is not the big, all-powerful person we had created for ourselves. If your therapist expresses concerns that the therapy is in trouble because of him, *listen.* As much as you might want to hang on to the relationship or the attachment, your therapist is doing you a great service by saying that he has gone as far as possible with you. It may be time to move on.

Sometimes therapy feels stuck because it isn't clear enough what you are working on. Wanting better self-esteem, for example, is a place to start when you first go for therapy. But without knowing what you have to work on, specifically, to achieve this, you probably won't feel much better. This is actually one of Sharon's problems, although she is so lost in her feelings that she cannot see it. Sharon wants to feel better through "love," and she never gets it because, as she is doing with Len, she looks for it in all the wrong places. When she can see that her goal should be to understand her behavior and to change it into something that is good for her instead of self-destructive, she will be heading in a positive direction.

Every therapy gets stuck now and then. This doesn't automatically mean that the therapist should be blamed or the therapy abandoned. But, if you feel stuck, then at that point, you are. Paying attention to this sense of not making any headway is crucial. Being active about it is just as crucial.

Unfortunately, we often assume that if something is going badly, it is our fault because we are bad or defective. This is a shameful and painful feeling, and by avoiding it we don't actively address our difficulty. We just hope that things will get better somehow. But this is a passive stance—a remnant from childhood when we *had* to depend on others. When we don't think about ourselves as powerful, we often wait for things to get better. Things may or may not get better on their own, but chances are they won't change much without our active help.

Quitting therapy at this point won't help much either, unless it's a clear, understood decision, made because this therapy isn't working for you. But just stopping will leave many conflicts and issues unresolved. Quitting may be avoiding something painful that could turn out to be the very reason you went into therapy in the first place.

And complaining about it will only help if you are complaining about it to your therapist. Talking to your friends about your dissatisfaction doesn't take the problem where it belongs. Of course it can be scary to talk about it with a therapist. How difficult it would be for Sharon to approach her adored Len with something like, "Len, this is really hard for me to say, but I have to say it. I've been coming here for six months now, and I realize that I don't actually feel any better." It doesn't sound like Sharon's style, does it? But if she did manage to tell Len her complaint, she would most likely hear something like, "That's very important to hear. Let's look at why that is." Or perhaps he would say, "I'm sorry that you still feel bad. We need to look at that. It's also interesting that it comes as a surprise to me. I wonder about that, too."

From such an opening, they could go on to understand how Sharon's need to please has kept her from sharing very much that is true. And it would now be possible for Sharon to understand her whole style of relating, with all of its negative consequences. But Sharon is too concerned about Len's good opinion to risk angering or upsetting him with her dissatisfaction. It's clear that trying to keep Len feeling good only keeps Sharon from changing.

Sharon's case is an extreme example of a common feeling. We don't want to risk the anger or disappointment of someone, like a therapist, who is so important to us. But it is vital to understand that the risk is definitely worth taking. It is amazing how many feelings get resolved simply by talking about them. If we hang on to them, they grow and fester; if we are open about them, we find that they are not so bad as we thought. This holds true whether you're confronting a therapist, a friend, or a relative. This kind of emotional risk-taking is vital to a good therapy.

The Therapist on a Pedestal

This leads us to another warning sign that a therapy is stuck, and definitely one that applies to Sharon: she puts her therapist on a pedestal. Think about what Sharon has said—she's concerned about what Len thinks of her all of the time and judges herself by whether or not she believes she's pleasing him. She dwells on her feelings for him and believes that the good feeling she has about him and with him is what will make her happy. None of this, of course, has anything to do with the work she is supposed to be doing with Len; it is all about how special she thinks he is.

This particular fantasy can lead to other kinds of fantasies and preoccupations. It's not uncommon to find yourself wanting to have a relationship with your therapist outside of therapy, to wish to become lovers or friends. There is nothing wrong with this—it's part of what happens when you trust someone with your feelings and that person is helping you. But it's important to talk about it, rather than keep it a secret. Keeping it a secret will affect your honesty, and therefore it will limit what you can achieve in therapy.

(It's important to note here that your therapist should never accede to your wishes to turn your therapy relationship into a love relationship or a friendship. Therapy should be a safe place to talk about your feelings without negative consequences. Your therapist will demonstrate his or her care and concern for you by *not* accepting your request for another kind of relationship.)

One of the hazards of thinking too much about your therapist as a love partner, and not dealing with what lies behind the desire, is that you may end up feeling you would be better if your therapist would just love you. Your therapy is then about getting your therapist to love you, instead of about growing and changing and getting better. This might well be Sharon's fate if she is unable to talk to Len about her feelings for him.

Sharon, like many people, assumes that her therapist knows how to make her life better. She has so idealized him that she ends up feeling her own solutions or insights are unimportant compared to his. She doesn't work on and value her own participation in the therapy; instead, she waits passively for her therapist to make her better.

Clearly, you can't put your therapist on a pedestal without putting yourself "down." If you give your therapist so much power, you will relinquish your own. You will have given up your own power in exchange for the fantasy that your therapist will save you. There are two clear reasons why this attitude will keep a therapy stuck. First, because he can't do your emotional work for you (and you certainly won't be doing the work if you're waiting for him to do it for you). Second, you will not strengthen and validate your own skills and resources, and that is what you are looking for in order to get better.

Keeping Secrets

When you realize that you are intentionally keeping secrets from your therapist, when you don't want to tell your therapist what you are thinking, and may have a very compelling reason for feeling this way, you are almost surely stuck. But you are going to stall your therapy if you stay in this place for very long.

Often these secrets are about things that fill you with shame. When they come up in therapy, you have the usual reaction to them: feel the shame and wish to hide them. But therapy is about questioning and exploring your usual reactions. Giving in to them will most likely keep you right where you are.

The feeling that the therapist will not like you or love you if you reveal what is true about you gets carried into therapy. As difficult as it is, you must confront and work to understand this feeling. Often the feeling of shame is there because of something bad that someone has done *to* you. And yet you are feeling the bad feelings that the *other* person ought to feel, not you. Sexual abuse of a child usually causes the child to feel shame. Yet, clearly, the child did nothing to be ashamed of. If you don't challenge your belief that you are to blame and have something to be ashamed of, then you will remain stuck in your therapy.

It is easy, in therapy, to be concerned that you are doing it right; you want to be a "good" client or patient. If you have thoughts or feelings that you think are bad, it is easy to assume that your therapist will feel the same way. You don't want to be a "bad" client, so you don't tell your "bad" thoughts. And then you perpetuate your belief that these thoughts and feelings are bad, with no evidence to the contrary.

It is common, too, to think that you won't have to tell what you are thinking. If the therapist gets to know you well enough, you hope she will eventually figure it out without your having to tell her. Perhaps she will ask just the right question, thus giving you the permission you're seeking to talk about this painful issue.

Sometimes, of course, this does happen. The picture starts to come into focus in the therapist's mind, and she asks the next obvious question and gets you off the hook. One of the wonderful things about therapy is that another person can know you so well that they can anticipate what is bothering you. But you can't depend on that. It may or may not happen. Waiting for it perpetuates your belief that you cannot express what you are thinking because it's wrong or bad. Waiting for your therapist to do the talking keeps you passive, and it keeps you stuck.

There are no promises or guarantees about how telling the truth will work. But, chances are, your therapist will not express horror, disgust, or even displeasure when she hears what you have been afraid to say. All your years of keeping it a secret have made it bad. Your therapist will probably be very sorry that it happened to you and will have little reaction beyond that. And from there, the two of you will go on to understand how this painful episode has affected you over the years and will look at ways to reduce the power it has over you.

Change requires risk. If you want therapy to work, you must have the courage to break the rules you've made for yourself about what is acceptable to talk about. As painful and frightening as this may be, it is not as bad as staying stuck.

What were the warning signs for Pam and Kathy that they were stuck? For Kathy, there were two clear warning signs. The first was that she *felt* stuck. Despite lots of work, much of what she came to get help with stayed just as it was. A sense of frustration was building in her. She assumed that this lack of movement was her fault, and as she blamed herself, she felt stupid and incompetent. This sense of frustration also started her thinking that maybe therapy couldn't work for her, and this gave her a frightening, hopeless feeling.

She was also keeping secrets. She had not actually forgotten that her father had sexually abused her or that he had been involved in criminal activities. But she had tucked these things away and had avoided thinking and talking about them. If she had kept those things perpetually secret, she never would have made much progress.

For Pam, the main warning signs were that she wanted her therapy to feel good and that she had put her therapist on a pedestal. She came to therapy with lots of hope, but the hope centered around her feeling that this therapist would both love her in the ways that she had wanted her mother to love her and tell her how to manage her life. She had to see that feeling good in therapy wasn't going to make her better, and that working to preserve that good feeling was a roadblock to change.

Pam and Kathy were stuck because they lived in denial about the realities of their lives. But they are not unusual. We all create certain fantasies for ourselves to cope with the inevitable frustrations, disappointments, and fears of childhood.

We go into therapy, however, because we want things to be different, and because the way we have been doing things hasn't been working. In the next chapter, we'll look at how therapy actually works. And in the second section of this book, we'll explain how to use your therapy to accomplish your goals and to find new and better ways to deal with old problems and pain.

— 6 —

How Therapy
Actually Works

Laura, age four, is in her bedroom crying. She just woke up, and her father is with her. She had brought home a special dessert from a dinner party, a marvelous concoction prepared by one of the guests, a professional pastry chef. Tired though she was, she gobbled it down when she got home, late at night, and she found the experience intensely pleasurable. "Umm, umm, yum—my!" she kept saying. She seems to have forgotten that she already ate it. "I want the one that we brought home last night," she wails.

Her dad is very empathic. He reminds her that she already ate it. She protests: She really wants it; she is very upset. But her father is calm and steady, and is able to soothe her. He doesn't become frustrated when she insists that the dessert is still there. He lets her be sad with him, and she starts to calm down. Her protests get quieter. He holds her. The crying stops; she's ready to move on.

That's what we want good therapy to do. Good therapists are with us when we are sad or hurt, and they allow us our pain. They help us with reality. They are there for us in a very real and comforting way. They help us deal with our loss. Through a combination of our working through our difficulties and their help and support, we get through our pain and end up in a new and better place.

Of course, this is our view. There are many theories about how different therapies work, and only a small amount of research has been done that is solid enough to prove anything. It can be very difficult to determine whether a therapy is good because it's new and better or bad because it's completely untested. Perhaps you want to trust something because it has stood the test of time. But maybe it's missing parts that are new, helpful, and important. How do you know where to turn? There are so many different points of view.

Different Theories and Different Therapies

Behavior therapists believe that if you change your behavior, your feelings (and often your thinking) will have to change along with it. This theory is behind some of the best techniques for dealing with fears and phobias. Behaviorists also believe that if you practice something often enough, it will become your automatic behavior. They believe that it matters little why you feel the way you do or how you got to be how you are. You must work in the present to change what is wrong now.

Cognitive therapists operate on the principle that if you change the way you think about something, your feelings and behavior will change to follow the change in thinking. The mind is moldable, or plastic. Through cognitive techniques, you can work to actually change your thinking habits. ("Bad things always happen to me," for example, could be changed to, "Life just has its ups and downs.") This theory is behind some of the best psychotherapy for depression. It is also an important part of treatment for addictions and all sorts of mal-adaptive behaviors.

Psychodynamic theories began with Freud. According to Freudian theory, what is hidden in the unconscious is as important as what is conscious. Jung diverged from Freud and began to work on ideas about the *collective unconscious*. He believed that our behaviors and our feelings reflect not only our individual selves, but also larger issues and deeper meanings about life and spirituality. Jungian therapists help their clients tap into their connection with universal issues and use their dreams to access their own unconscious knowledge about themselves.

Freudian theorists believe that our unconscious conflicts and unacceptable impulses exert powerful control over us. They block us from growing because our energy is spent keeping those unconscious forces at bay. The job of therapy, then, is to discover what is unconscious and learn to accept it, thereby releasing this blockage of our emotional life.

Object relations theory looks at how we are affected by the particular ways we are treated in our early relationships. It is a strange name for a therapy that focuses so exclusively on relationships, but the "objects" in object relations theory are actually people. This theory looks at early mothering and at very profound issues of connection and attachment. Object relations therapy aims to address troubles that arise in those early relationships.

Family systems theory deals with the impact of family dynamics on the individual. The theory deals with how an individual is shaped by the dynamics of her or his particular family. The therapy deals with understanding those dynamics and changing the family system.

There are certainly many more theories that are less prominent. Some are spiritual, some are interpersonal, some are physical. Many therapies deal with the body. According to these therapies, working with the body through direct physical intervention or through understanding the meaning of certain physical sensations should help us move through what is causing our pain. These therapies can be extremely helpful in dealing with physical or emotional trauma.

Our own training began with modern Freudian theory. This gave us a solid background in understanding the dynamics of the unconscious. But we quickly moved away from that and into our current work involving the psychology of women. Classical Freudian theory misses, or ignores, many issues for women. In fact, in Freud's famous quote "What do women want?" he was acknowledging his lack of understanding of women. His theories, even modern elaborations of them, have some big and important gaps in an understanding of women's psyche.

As we delved deeper into the psychology of women, we learned about the different dynamics in relationships for women compared to those for men, and we began to integrate different parts of our training into our work. In too many cases for women, classical Freudian therapy didn't work. Object relations theorists offered more relevant things to say about women and their development because of their focus on early relationships. Theories about the psychology of women were becoming more prominent, and many of these theories examined women from the perspective of women themselves. This was in exciting contrast to older theories, which were written by men, and which studied men as subjects, then described women as people who didn't behave in quite the same way as men!

We were fortunate enough to participate in the Denver Women Psychiatrists' Study Group, an independent group of women psychiatrists who gathered together to learn what we weren't taught in standard training. Supportive techniques, cognitive and behavioral techniques, body work, and other movement or expressive therapy became important to us. As a result of this new training, we became convinced that therapy groups for women were vitally important. Our exploration led us to create the Denver Women's Center, where we would put these theories into action.

Our own view of how therapy works comes from what would have to be called an eclectic perspective: we use different parts of different theories, believing there is much of value in many of them. No one theory makes the other theories obsolete. But perhaps because of our early training, we do value theories that deal with making the unconscious conscious. We do believe that the parts of us that remain hidden from ourselves have the potential to exert great power over our emotions and actions, and we believe that we all have feelings, thoughts, and behaviors of which we are unaware. Our therapy operates on the theory that knowing about and accepting what is real for ourselves is key to gaining emotional strength and freedom.

Is It the Theory or the Therapist?

How important is theory in a good therapy? There is a body of research that suggests that it doesn't matter whether the therapy is cognitive-behavioral, Jungian analysis, Freudian analysis, hypnotherapy, dance therapy, or psychodrama. According to many studies, the helpful part of therapy is what happens between the therapist and the client.

You didn't learn about who you are and what you feel in a vacuum. You learned these things in your relationships with the important people in your life. Their reactions and behaviors reflected yourself back to you, and so you learned who you are largely from them. There is something necessary, then, about doing this kind of work with another person. Much of what you can repair about how you feel about yourself, you must do in a new relationship.

A special connection exists between therapist and patient that gets made in therapy and that can promote healing. We are aware that we may sound as though we are talking out of both sides of our mouths. Didn't we just say that the relationship can be a trap? Yes, we did. But we also said that how we use the relationship is important; it can be a vital piece of what makes therapy work. So what exactly is this healing force? It isn't any one thing, but rather a combination of things that make it so special.

First of all is the common intention you both bring to the relationship: both of you have come together for the purpose of getting one of you well. By getting together with a therapist, you have found someone who, at least for the time that you are together, is working, just as you are, to help you change by listening to you, by trying to understand you, and by caring about you. The two of you are in a relationship that doesn't happen all that often in life, and it allows you to come together in ways that people usually don't. Most obviously, for example, you don't have to think about the therapist's needs or problems. You never have to say, "Well, that's enough about me. How about you?" You can be totally self-absorbed and have this other person center on you. This gives you the opportunity to open up to yourself and to take your issues more seriously than you ever have in the past. And you have the agreement of the therapist that he is there to take these issues seriously along with you.

You have listened to your own voice and your own thoughts long enough, and it hasn't helped, and now you have someone who is skilled at listening and understanding, someone who is there to hear the things that you're not hearing, and that person is there to tell you, as tactfully and as helpfully as possible, what she notices about you.

Gradually, you experience the therapist's support, guidance, and understanding. You build a sense of trust that allows you to go deeper into yourself and risk more and more. This trust allows you to try out the therapist's ideas when they are different from your own. This trust allows you to share secrets that you have been keeping all of your life. This trust is important in building hope because your therapist believes that you can do better for yourself and feel better about yourself. You are willing to accept that your therapist sees possibilities for you that you cannot see for yourself.

From this trust comes safety. This is a key to progress in therapy, because a feeling of undefined danger leads us to build up many of our defenses, and a feeling of safety lets us begin to break them down. This safety allowed the four-year-old Laura to let her father help her. She felt safe enough to listen to him and to let him soothe her. Allowing him to guide her through her difficulty allowed her to feel better herself. She mastered a loss and became just a little bit stronger for having done so. Without trust and safety, her upset would have gone on much longer, probably ending because she had cried herself out, not because she had resolved anything.

This empathic connection, understanding, trust, and safety provide a place where it is safe to risk, grow, and change. It is not sufficient in itself to produce much change without more active work.

Learning What the Real Work Is

The therapy relationship is the context in which the work of therapy can get done. Laura didn't feel better just because her father held her. She felt better because she did some real psychological work. She had to accept her loss. It was a small loss in the scheme of the things, but at the moment, to Laura, it was enormous. There was nothing she wanted more, when she woke up in the morning, than to enjoy that wonderful pastry all over again. Her whole self was focused on it. So when it wasn't there, it was a *big* disappointment. There was no sweet treat; it was gone. That was the reality of the moment, and the work that Laura did was to grieve its loss.

Grieving constitutes much of the work of therapy. That is Pam's work, and that is Kathy's work. Pam must grieve the loss of the kind mothering she never had. The dynamics established between her and her mother affected her throughout her life, hurting her badly and causing her pain. She is angry and disappointed about how it was for her. Her work is accepting that reality as well as accepting all of the feelings that go along with it. Until she grieves it, she can't let it go, and she keeps replaying her old fantasies, trying to make it different.

Pam's not grieving her reality would be like Laura crying and insisting that there really was another pastry in the kitchen and being angry that her father wouldn't give it to her. As long as Pam insisted that her mother really was good at loving, she could stay sad and angry that she wasn't getting any of that love, but when she grieved that there wasn't much love to have, she was able to move on.

Kathy has to grieve about the real harm that was done to her as an innocent child. And she has to grieve about how unsafe her family was. As long as she refuses to do this, she only continues to hate herself.

The real work is real work! And it is work that the therapist cannot do for you. You have to do it for yourself. The therapist can definitely help by helping you understand what has to be grieved. ("There is no more pastry.") In this way, the therapist is your ally in breaking through the denial and in sticking with the reality. This is a whole lot of help, even though it feels bad because the reality causes the pain. But at least now it is possible for you to get through it and put it behind you.

Getting through the pain is an important part of the work, and the therapist can be the "holding environment" while you do it. The therapist can coach you and guide you as you do your work, but the work is about change, and change includes pain. So the therapy is not just about soothing you. It is about soothing you enough so that you don't feel too alone or too afraid with your pain. It is about soothing you enough so that you feel support and hope, and have the courage to take the next step.

Part II

The Solutions

— 7 —

Achievable Goals
for Therapy

Why is Cinderella such an enduring and compelling story? And Sleeping Beauty? And Snow White? The beautiful young women in these stories lived happily ever after (after the right man came along, that is!). And while they waited, perhaps they scrubbed the floors, or did other peoples' laundry, or just slept!

We've grown up with these myths, these fantasies, and it is no surprise that searching for love, for many women, has become an end in itself. If we get someone to love us, we have learned, everything will be all right. In therapy, as in other relationships, many women try to get the love and approval of the therapist. But the more we focus on getting this "love" from outside ourselves, the more we ignore the inside.

Our message about making therapy work for you is that the therapist, as deeply as she may care for you, is not there to love you. Trying to win your therapist's love is *not only an unachievable goal for therapy, it is an unproductive one.* There are far more productive goals to aim for.

In this chapter, we will address three productive goals that can be achieved in therapy.

1. Distinguishing the past from the present.
2. Gaining real control.
3. Distinguishing between good pain and bad pain.

Goal Number One: Distinguishing the Past From the Present

We have to know what is true about the past in order to be able to tell the difference between it and the present. Let us say this again because it is, perhaps, the most important point of this book. *We have to know what is true about the past in order to be able to tell the difference between it and the present.* Many, many problems arise from denying the truth about the past.

It follows that we have to be willing to admit that the past still affects us in the present. We must be open to the possibility that the way we see things in the present may be distorted and inaccurate, and that we are bringing too much of our past experience into the present. Clearly, our first realistic and appropriate goal for therapy is to learn to distinguish the past from the present.

Now that we've said that, we also need to add that this is not necessarily easy to accomplish because of our natural wish to deny the pain from our past. But it can be done, and it is one of the ways that therapy can be truly helpful. As we explore this goal, we will look at two problems that result from confusing the past with the present. These problems often lead to unhappiness in peoples' lives, unhappiness that brings them to therapy. The first is the repetition of maladaptive or self-destructive patterns of behavior from the past. The second is the transference of feelings from past relationships onto present ones.

If You Love Me, I'll Feel Better

Even though Pam entered therapy to deal with depression and an eating disorder, Pam's goal in therapy now centers on getting her therapist to love her. Pam (who we should know fairly well by now!) doesn't believe it yet, but getting her therapist to love her won't fix anything in her life. Yet earning that love has become the focus of her therapy, because she craves that feeling of being loved so badly that it can easily override any other thought or feeling. Feeling unloved is a terrible state to be in, and Pam experiences a great deal of pain about it. And it is the pain of being unloved on which she focuses, even obsesses.

Trying to prove she is lovable is behavior that would have made sense if it had happened in the past (that is, with her mother), but it doesn't make much sense in the present. It was her fantasy from childhood that she could get her mother to love her. And even though it never worked, and even though that chapter in her life is over and done with, she continues to hope for that special love. This repetition of behavior from her past is understandable, given the trouble we all have letting go of our childhood fantasies.

We do have trouble letting go. The human mind has a propensity to learn things quickly and yet to unlearn them very slowly. As we said earlier, sometimes it seems as if we aren't even as smart as a rat in a maze. A rat in a maze, when looking for cheese, will go down one path, and once he finds the cheese will continue to look for it in that same place. But if the next few times it isn't there, the rat will search out the smell of the cheese and then look for the cheese where the smell is. It won't go down the same empty path when it can smell cheese somewhere else.

We, on the other hand, just seem to go down the same path over and over again. If it worked in the past, we just keep doing it. As a child, Pam learned that it made her feel better to hope for her mother to love her, and now she doesn't know how to stop hoping.

We try to rework the past in the present. Without realizing it, we hope that if we can make it work now, today, then we won't have to grieve the past. We hope we can avoid that pain.

So now, in her same familiar way, Pam hopes people will love her. That's her thing, to repeat behavior from the past. She believes that she must work to be loved, and yet, at the same time, she believes that she will never achieve that goal, that she will never be loved. Whoever gets into a close relationship with her gets caught in this game. No matter how much someone may care for her, she can't believe in their love. She believes, instead, that she will be disappointed, and waits for that disappointment as much as she waits for the love. In essence, she *transfers* her experience of her past relationships onto her present relationships. *Transference*, then, is one of the ways in which we repeat the past. Let's look more closely at how this works.

Transference

Franny had a father who was attractive and charming. He was also a gambler and a cheat. When she was little, she just adored her father—he was fun, he took her out, he made her feel very special, and he loved to give her surprises and treats.

It wasn't until she was older that she learned that the special gifts from her dad were bought with borrowed money, money that he believed he would recoup through gambling. Of course, like most gamblers, he usually lost more money than he made, and he sank deeper and deeper into debt. This strained his marriage, and life at home was fraught with tension. But Franny always forgave her father, for he always showered her with love and praise and made her feel wonderful.

So, what does Franny do now, as an adult, when she finds herself attracted to a man? For one thing, she tends to bypass men of substance, and tends to be attracted to a man's external charm, sex appeal, and flattery. She ignores any warning signs that he may be unreliable or manipulative, and she's very good at it, since she spent her childhood learning to ignore the transgressions of a charming man.

Even though she ignores the warning signs that a man is not going to really come through for her, she still feels the potential for disaster, but on an unconscious level. So even though she may happily fall in love, she also feels a kind of insecurity and doubt—a generalized darkness of spirit. She knows on a deep level that she is not truly safe. But since that is a familiar feeling, it does not alarm her, even though it actually feels bad. She is used to it, and she doesn't know any other way to feel.

That's how she does relationships now: she transfers her experience with her father onto her relationships with other men. She is easily caught by any man's superficial charm. And though she tries to develop intimate relationships with her various lovers, she carries with her an underlying doubt that any man is ever going to come through for her. She thinks she is seeing each man as an individual, but she doesn't have a clue how to go about finding out what a man is really like. Instead she sees him through the lens of her past experience and her expectations.

When she does get involved with someone who can be trustworthy and serious, the relationship falls apart. She can't maintain a relationship with a loving and honest man. She may date a man because she thinks she should, but she doesn't feel the same kind of passionate attraction to him, and, basically, she thinks he's boring!

Transference, then, is the transferring of feelings experienced in one relationship onto another, and usually the transferring of the dynamics of a past relationship onto a present one. The relationship in the present is then dealt with as if it were one from the past. The old relationship, in essence, gets repeated.

Once this transfer is made, it tends to lose the "as if" quality and becomes real. For example, when Franny gets involved with a nice man, she doesn't think to herself, "Gee, isn't it funny that I keep thinking this nice guy has nothing to offer me? I guess I'm just looking for someone more like my father." Instead she thinks, "He seems nice, and we had a little fun, but I need someone more exciting."

We don't consider transference something we, ourselves, have created. To us, it's a reality—*our* reality, of course, but our reality from the past. And it is very difficult to shake our belief that it is also the reality of the present. Despite the diversity of our present relationships, despite all the opportunities for different kinds of relationships, we tend to do them all the same. We learn to do this dance, to play this game, as though we were still children. We become masters at it, and we just keep playing it. This transference from the past leads to repetition of patterns from the past.

Pam plays her transference out with her therapist. Once she begins to care about her, she begins to make her over into her mother. The pattern she lays on the relationship is that in order to feel better, she has to try hard to get her therapist to love her. And she will show that she does, in different ways, from time to time. But Pam expects never to feel secure, or truly cared for, in this relationship. It doesn't matter who her therapist really is; she relates to her as if she were someone who (like her mother) can care minimally, when treated properly, but in whose love or care she can never feel secure.

This is all she knows how to do. It didn't get her what she needed in the past. And it doesn't do her any good in the present. It only keeps her stuck, repeating the same old dance, unconsciously, perpetually.

We all do the dance of transference. It's normal and it's natural, but it's also unconscious. And as long as it is unconscious, it affects us without our knowing about it. We repeat our old relationships without conscious awareness, and if those relationships were at all destructive, we risk repeating that destructiveness in our present. In order to change and to grow, we need to make our actions conscious; then, we are in control.

If we had loving, trusting parents, and we get involved with loving, trusting people who treat us well, then the transference issue is less cause for problems in our present. But if there are destructive patterns of behavior from our early years that we repeat unconsciously rather than understand, those past patterns cause us real trouble in the present.

Often, as in Kathy's case, understanding the transference can be the first light shed on a hidden truth. Kathy, as we stated earlier, had a fantasy that preserved her sense of a safe childhood but that simultaneously destroyed her sense of herself. She believed, basically, that she was the bad one. Her belief was that her family was good and that if she had been good, she would have felt good within the family. But in her mind, she caused trouble, she was moody, and she ruined everyone else's good time. The problems she had were, therefore, because of trouble that she herself made or because of how she reacted to things. (Many people from abusive families have been labeled as "too sensitive" and go through life believing that this sensitivity is a real character flaw.)

Whenever such people feel bad about something, they figure their feelings are wrong. If someone around them is unhappy (about anything) they assume they are the cause of that unhappiness. For Kathy, her responsibility for other peoples' bad feelings is all-encompassing. Her sense of her own badness invades every area of her life and every relationship.

Naturally, then, this feeling about herself comes with her to the therapy relationship as well. While she goes to therapy for help, she has a difficult time thinking that the therapist might actually like her, care about her, or be on her side. Instead, she thinks of her as someone who tolerates her, who is basically as critical of her as she is of herself, but who acts kindly because she's being paid for her time.

In this relationship between "bad" patient and "good" but critical therapist, all Kathy can hope for is to be tolerated. Because she believes she is bad, she believes that others see her as bad as well. That is her past experience, which she superimposes on the present. Everything is seen through this filter, and her therapy will be no different. (The difference is that in therapy, these feelings can be challenged.)

Kathy has a lifetime of experience in making anything that happens fit her belief system. So, for example, if the therapist expresses true kindness, warmth, or caring that Kathy can feel, she might say to herself, "Well, that's what she thinks now, but when she learns a little more about me, she'll change her mind about me." Or if she gets some real help, she might think, "Well, that was nice, but it won't happen again . . . I won't count on it."

This system is so complete within itself that nothing nice can ever be seen for what it is; everything gets interpreted through her belief in her badness. Since this is her reality, good things become, for her, either fakes or temporary aberrations.

This can drive a therapist a little crazy! You may think that we therapists don't become involved personally in our work, but that is far from the truth. When our feelings and motives are misinterpreted, we notice; if the client sees us as rejecting and judgmental when, in fact, we feel empathic and supportive, eventually we're forced to say something about it. This is often where we can be most helpful and where some of the most important work of therapy takes place.

Kathy's therapist had to point out this misinterpretation of her own motives over and over again. Just once won't convince someone like Kathy, because it takes work for such a radically different idea to take root. In Kathy's situation, her therapist had to point out Kathy's misinterpretations many times because it had been so important to Kathy to see herself as bad.

She met her therapist's alternative view of her with considerable resistance, but at least she did struggle with the new ideas. The dialogue between them may have gone something like this:

"You seem distant to me right now," her therapist told her.

"Well, I don't want to feel your disapproval."

"What disapproval is that," her therapist said gently.

Kathy was not sure she wanted to answer truthfully, but at last she said, "About what I did this weekend."

"But I don't disapprove," the therapist said. "In fact,
I think I understand why you did what you did."

Kathy looked suspicious.

"That's difficult to believe, isn't it?" said the therapist.

Kathy listened to what her therapist said, and then she
debated it. Her therapist said something nice, and she rejected
it. When her therapist took her side, she got angry.

But most important, when her therapist challenged Kathy to
dispute her reality, Kathy agreed to the challenge. When she
saw, eventually, that she had only one way to see all relationships, and when her therapist refused to participate in that kind
of relationship (that is, refused to criticize and punish Kathy),
Kathy had a real opportunity. She could leave therapy because
it was too uncomfortable. And she could tell herself that this
therapist obviously doesn't know what she's doing. Or she could
tolerate the conflict within herself that came from her therapist's interventions and pay attention to what she (Kathy) did
within the therapy relationship.

Fortunately, Kathy chose the latter path. In responding to
her therapist's challenge to her belief system, she began to see
that she was superimposing one experience onto another, that
she was living in the present as if it were the past, and that she
went on repeating the old patterns over and over again.

This is difficult but rewarding work for both therapist and
client, and a fair example of what can be done in therapy in
order to change your life. Notice that Kathy is not going to get
well just by getting her therapist to love her. If anything, she'll
get better by seeing just how much she doesn't believe that her
therapist even *can* love her. She is going to get well by seeing
how she is unconsciously repeating her past relationships in the
present. And it is through working in therapy that she can discover what she has hidden from herself (that is, what has been
unconscious) and bring it into the light of awareness.

Notice, too, how important the therapy relationship is to this
work. But, rather than working for the therapist's love, the client

needs to work for rapport, trust, empathy, and understanding. These are the tools that make the transference work possible. Love is not the goal.

Dealing with transference repetition in the therapy relationship is a powerful step toward recognizing that the present is different from the past, but there are other ways this can happen in therapy. If we are willing to look at the past, and not to continually turn away from it, we can use therapy to go back in time and to better understand feelings and conflicts that have grown out of early events and situations in our lives. Using the therapist as our sounding board, guide, or trusted objective partner in this effort, we can make great progress in clarifying who we are and where we come from.

Like most of us, Kathy was unaware of how her behavior in the present reflected her past, but through informed questions and observations, her therapist could illuminate the links between today and yesterday. As an example, Kathy brought into one session a story that dealt with her anger and disappointment in her husband for dismissing her wish to return to school. "How did he tell you this?" asked the therapist. "He didn't have to tell me in words. I knew from how he stomped around the house," Kathy replied. "Perhaps he was stomping about something else," the therapist said, and then continued, "Can you ask him what he's upset about?" Kathy looked a little surprised. "I didn't think I had to. I knew he was mad at me."

Since we are outside observers, we can see that Kathy has made an assumption about her husband. But why does she do this? At this point, the therapist might wonder with her, "Does this remind you of how you used to feel as a little girl? If someone felt bad, was it always your fault?" Chances are, Kathy would reply, "Always. It was always my fault."

Kathy's current distress is evidence of her past reality. Her therapist is teaching her how to be curious about her feelings and reactions, because the drama of her past is often played out in the present. As a trusted partner, a therapist can help you find clues in your present to what happened in your past.

If we deny the past, we cannot possibly learn from it, or even distinguish it from the present. In the familiar words of George Santayana, "Those who cannot remember the past are condemned to repeat it."

The result of being able to distinguish the past from the present is freedom and choice. Freedom comes because of the whole range of possibilities that is opened up when we don't have to repeat the past; choice comes because once we can see what we are doing, we can chose whether or not to do it.

Please notice that none of this depends on the therapist loving or even liking us. It depends only on two people being able to work honestly together. We have said—and we will repeat—that this is difficult work. But it is work worth doing.

Goal Number Two: Gaining Real Control

Fantasies don't work; reality does. So achievable goal number two is to learn where we have *real* control. This is difficult for women because it means centering on ourselves and our own needs: it means focusing on ourselves. We are terrified of this. Having been taught all our lives that we will be rejected or even hated for being "selfish," we often think that we will lose everything and everybody if we work for ourselves.

Where Do Women Take Control?

We were writing this chapter during the Christmas season. What a time to think about women's cultural roles and the expectations we have of ourselves! What are the holidays but a time when a woman's job is to make everyone's wishes come true? Men may assemble the bikes and trains, but it's women who keep track of what everyone wants. We exist to please. We secretly hope that someone will also think about us, and sometimes it works out that way. But, more often, we emerge from the holidays, if we can look at it honestly, depleted and disappointed. And we feel this way because we have worked so hard to make everyone else happy—a magnification of what we usually do.

Men have learned to go out into the world and to achieve their goals using whatever power and control they can muster to do so, but we women have been taught not to be so "self-centered." Jean Baker Miller writes in her book, *Toward a New Psychology of Women,* that "Women have different organizing principles around which their psyches are structured. One of these principles is that they exist to serve other peoples' needs." In addition to the cultural requirement that women meet others' needs, many women also have to meet the more specific emotional needs of their parents. They think that they have to, and they think that they can!

When a child has to work to create the fantasy of a safe and loving environment in the midst of a dangerous and unpredictable one, she often works to figure out what will make things safe. One way to do this is to tune in to her parents' emotional states and to try to do whatever she can to make them feel okay. Her whole emotional life, then, becomes focused on other peoples' emotions. She thinks she will get her own emotional needs met by fulfilling the emotional needs of others.

How do you meet your own needs when your first priority is to meet other peoples' needs? Well, it's a tricky business. In essence, you have to do it indirectly. You meet other peoples' needs first, but you try to allow some room for yourself in the process. Or you give to others what you hope is enough so that they will be moved to reciprocate. You hope to get something for yourself without asking for it directly, and you hope that others will figure out what you need, just as you try to figure out what they need. Sometimes this becomes so natural that you automatically focus on others, as if that is what you actually need. And sometimes you try to (forgive the word, but it is accurate) manipulate others into giving you what you want.

"Manipulate" is a nasty word. Nobody thinks manipulation is a nice thing. And it's a word that is often used together with the word "woman." It is hardly a surprise, though, that women are manipulative, since indirect means are often the only ones available to them. As long as we are not out there getting what we want for ourselves, we don't have to be seen by others or see ourselves as selfish, and, therefore, unfeminine. No, we have permission to get what we need if we aren't too direct or aggressive in getting it.

So, if we don't have permission to get what we need and want for ourselves, and are allowed to get what we need only if someone else decides it's okay for us to have it and gives it to us, is it any surprise that we go about getting what we want by trying to control other people?

"Controlling" is certainly another word that is often used together with "woman." Ironically, it is because we *lack control* in the world that we try to take control in other ways.

All of us know (we hope!) that we can't really control other people; no one wants to be controlled. So, in our attempts to control our world through others, we are doomed to frustration, doomed to a sense that we lack control. It's a vicious cycle: the harder we try, the more resistance we get, and the more resistance we get, the harder we try. And, since it is all that is allowed us, we just keep trying harder and harder to make it work.

Pseudocontrol

Women become masters at creating ways to gain some sort of control, but that have nothing, really, to do with getting what we need. We have found arenas in which we think we have control. So we work in these areas, imagining that we are having real control over our lives. We (the authors) call this *pseudocontrol.*

Pseudocontrol takes infinite forms, but there are some common themes. Controlling our world through controlling others may be the main one. For example, if we had an unpredictable, moody mother, we become good at tuning in to another's emotional needs. So we may marry a volatile, irrational man, and we think, "If I can keep him calm, he'll be able to love me." Or we may think that our obligation in life is to make sure that we never offend anyone, and only then can we be considered acceptable. We try to orchestrate our interactions with other people so that they turn out just right for everyone. Each of these examples takes a huge amount of energy and is, of course, doomed to failure since we don't have that much actual control over anyone else. It's a fantasy that we do—one that served us well in childhood but that wastes our lives in the present.

Sometimes we bend all our efforts in an attempt to control our physical environment. Maybe we think we need a new sofa before the big dinner party, or we have to get the right color of geraniums before they're sold out at the garden shop. Perhaps we feel temporary relief when the kitchen floor is spotless or the playroom is picked up—temporary relief of a nameless anxiety. But if we don't deal with what we really need or what we really need control of, the anxiety will come back quickly because its root has been ignored. And the whole thing starts again, this time perhaps with birthday party plans or getting just the right message on the Christmas cards.

The fantasy involved in trying to gain control by controlling the physical world might include a preoccupation with appearance: "If I look pretty enough," we bargain, "then the right man will love me," or even, "If I look pretty enough, everyone will love me." Or it might be, "If I look stylish, people will like and respect me."

We can spend a lifetime attending to these goals—we can work on our hair, makeup, and clothing. We can read fashion magazines and spend lots of time shopping for just the right shoes or belt. No matter how much time and effort (and money!) we put into this, we still wonder if we are loved or respected. But because we believe that this is how we will get what we need, we keep plugging away. This process gives us the sense of control, but the control is only an illusion.

We use this kind of false control, or pseudocontrol, when we don't have any other way to have genuine control over what is important to us. No matter how unproductive our methods may actually be, having something that we can do is better than feeling there is nothing that we can do. When we were children and had no power, the fantasy of control was all we had.

As adults, we actually have more options and, therefore, more real control. Since we're repeating old childhood patterns and hanging on to old childhood beliefs, however, we still *feel* as if we don't have real control. As adult women, the task of identifying and using our real control is particularly difficult because we have been taught by our culture not to take control for ourselves.

Pam, for example, works overtime trying to get people to love her. She goes out of her way to do nice things for people. She doesn't ask too much for herself so as not to appear selfish. She adheres to a very high code of morals and ethics, and hopes always to do what's right and good. Does all of this determine whether or not people will love her? Of course not. She has no real control over whether they actually love her or not. Either they'll love her or they won't. As a child, she couldn't possibly have tolerated the feeling that her mother didn't love her, so she escaped that feeling by her belief, her fantasy, that she had control over her mother's love. If only she did this, that, or the other thing, then her mother would love her. She brings that fantasy into the present and works at this, that, or the other thing for everybody, including her therapist, trying to make them love her by trying to control their feelings for her.

This method is bound to backfire. For one thing, no matter how much her therapist cares for her, that love and caring in itself can't heal the old wounds. Until Pam does the hard work of healing those wounds, the therapist's love will never feel as though it's enough.

In addition, we all know how unpleasant it is to be with someone who is disappointed in us, or seems needy (that is, needing more than we can give). Yet that is how Pam often seems to others. Although prepared to care for and get involved with her, many keep their distance because they get the feeling when they're with Pam that something's not right between them. The comfort level required for sharing and intimacy doesn't get established. Pam ends up feeling rejected and unloved.

If Pam were trying only to control what she can actually control (that is, herself) she would be immensely likable and would have more friends than she'd know what to do with. In truth, she's bright, warm, funny, friendly, open, empathic, thoughtful, and honest. Who wouldn't want someone like that for a friend? Who wouldn't love that person?

In learning to have real control, we have to be willing to accept that there are things we cannot affect, despite our desire to do so. We call this a *developmental task* of adulthood. If it rains during the company picnic that you spent six months planning, you feel lousy. If your niece dies of leukemia, you grieve. If your boss has a transference reaction to you and is never satisfied with your work no matter how well you do, you can't change that. It doesn't mean that you have to like the situation; you simply go ahead and do the best that you can, look for support from your coworkers, and decide if you must look for another job. But it is important to deal with what is real. If you try using pseudocontrol instead, then you think that you ought to be able to influence your boss to be different. Since that clearly isn't possible, you might find yourself thinking about what a failure you are, what a bad person you are, or how nothing you do ever works out right.

The Alcoholics Anonymous "Serenity Prayer" captures our point well:

> *God grant me the serenity to accept the things I cannot change, the courage to change the things I can, and the wisdom to know the difference.*

It's amazing how much extra energy we have when we're only working on areas in which we can actually have an effect. It feels so good when we stop beating our heads against the wall. When we accept what is real, we are in a position to use all of our potential strengths and resources.

This kind of acceptance may be difficult, however, because we have to face a painful reality, and we will have to deal with pain, loss, sadness, or whatever other feeling may go with that reality. Because of our natural resistance to dealing with what is painful and sad, we often need support and reassurance from someone else, usually a therapist, that it is worth it to feel that sadness and loss with the promise of future gain in emotional health.

We are often sad when we change our beliefs about what we can and cannot do because we have to give up our long-held fantasies, our treasured beliefs about how the world should be. And we are sad because accepting our limits involves loss, and loss brings sadness. But we wouldn't push so strongly to do this if there were not a huge payoff. The payoff is being able to enjoy reality, to enjoy life in the present.

Goal Number Three: Distinguishing Between Good Pain and Bad Pain

Learning to tell the difference between good pain and bad pain will change your life. It is such a powerful and simple lesson that, once you discover its power and effectiveness, you will want to practice it daily to keep yourself on track by working to change what you can and to grieve what you can't.

Loss and Acceptance

We must talk about loss, although we would always prefer to avoid the subject. Much therapy doesn't work because we refuse to feel loss and pain. But change requires loss, because in order to have one thing, we must give up another.

It is perplexing that we resist *losing* something painful; on the surface, we would always prefer to lose something that causes us pain. The main point of this book is to understand why we hang on to pain and to demonstrate how to let it go.

In Chapter Three, we talked about good pain and bad pain. We said that bad pain is the pain that supports our childhood fantasies. It's bad not because it feels bad (as all pain does to some extent) but because of the *kind* of bad feeling it is: it is the kind of bad feeling that is relentless and ever present, the kind of pain that, *no matter how much you feel it, doesn't make anything better.* Good pain is good because it is part of the process of change. It is the pain of loss and of grieving, and it is good because it accomplishes something. Good pain is the pain not only of grief, but also of progress, growth, and change.

It is not easy, at first, to tell the difference between these two kinds of pain. Depression and anxiety are painful, bulimia is painful, and hopelessness and helplessness are painful. Remembering that you felt abandoned as a child is painful, recognizing that your father was abusive is painful, and knowing that your mother was never able to love you is painful. What is the difference? Pain is pain, right? No, it's not. There is a world of difference.

Central to the difference between good pain and bad pain is that *good pain is about something real that can be grieved. Bad pain is the result of a fantasy,* and is like a tape loop: it repeats over and over again and *it never changes.*

Kathy is so used to her bad pain that, although she goes to therapy so that it will get better, she doesn't think that it ever will. She hopes only that she will learn how to tolerate it better. Kathy's fantasy is that she was the bad one in her family. That fantasy made her parents seem as if they were good, which is a very big payoff for a child. The cost of her fantasy? She thinks she is bad. Her bad pain comes from this and spreads into every area of her life. She has low self-esteem. She doesn't pursue her goals because she doubts her competence. She feels unlovable. She gets depressed, and sometimes suicidal. She tries to drown her feelings in alcohol and food, and then feels even worse about herself after a binge.

This bad pain is the old, familiar one that goes away, perhaps, temporarily, but always returns in full force. It's always the same, and it feels relentless. It protects her from the other pain of recognizing how abandoned she was, emotionally, in childhood, and how abused she was by her father. When she thinks about that reality, which she is able to do, bit by bit, with the help of her therapist, she feels an entirely new kind of pain. It is the sharp pain of loss, combined with a profound sadness about how little this poor innocent girl she once was got out of life. She feels rage at her father, and that her mother betrayed her.

It's understandable that she has wanted to move away from this pain, and she would probably continue doing so if she didn't have a therapist to help her stay with the reality of her early life. She has noticed that each time she revisits this kind of pain with her therapist, it is a little different. Though she is afraid that she will feel unbearably sad forever, she actually feels this only for a short time. She learns that it is bearable, that she can tolerate it. Each time she feels the real pain of her childhood, she has the opportunity to grieve, and grieving is the process that moves us through our pain.

Our psychological work, as adults, usually is to deal with what happened to us when we were children. The clearest and most dramatic examples are often those of clear abuse or neglect. But there are many other aspects of our childhood that we must deal with that may be no one's fault but that still caused us trouble. Perhaps we moved eight times during our school years because our father was in the military, and we were always having to make new friends. Perhaps a sibling died or was still-born, and our parents' overwhelming grief made them unavailable to us as we tried to deal with our own sense of that loss. Perhaps we lived in a neighborhood that was extremely racist, and because we didn't understand the meaning of racism at the time, we just thought no one liked us. Perhaps we had parents who were very poor until our younger siblings were born, and we watched with confusion and envy as they got all the luxuries and advantages that we never had. These are issue that we must come to grips with as we grow as adults.

When we are alone and small, the real pain is often too difficult to face. We are still growing and developing, so we don't have the abilities we will have later on to help us cope. We may have been alone in our pain, as Kathy was. And we might have been in a terrible situation, like Kathy's, that was impossible to face. Like Kathy, we built up defenses to ward off this reality and to deny it. But we have the opportunity to grow by dealing with it as adults because we are no longer caught in the helplessness of childhood.

Grieving

Grieving is the process that can ultimately heal most of what we suffer in life. It's a process that does its work, slowly and naturally, as long as nothing interrupts it. When we grieve, we usually experience sadness and anger. Often, with a profound loss, we have difficulty believing in our loss, and we don't know how we will go on. But, gradually, new things come into our lives. We learn that we can go on; we learn to live with our sadness. When something is so overwhelming that it must be denied, though, the grieving process is interrupted. That is what happens to us as helpless children. Perhaps we are not in a safe place to grieve because we don't have support and validation. Perhaps it is because we don't have the internal strength to do this grieving. We are too little and, in the case of abuse, too alone.

But as adults, we can do our grief work. Therapy can be the place where we are able to do this, where we are no longer alone with our pain. And what we find, when we have the courage to go through our pain, is that, contrary to what we may have thought, we *can* do it!

When we do our grief work, we find that the pain we feel will lessen. That is what makes it good pain: it makes a positive difference in our lives if we let ourselves feel it. It is not needless pain and suffering; it is normal and appropriate pain, and it can diminish over time.

But let us give you some tips on how to make the grief work go better. Since it is difficult and painful, it works best when it's paced, and done one step at a time.

First of all, it helps to deal with the general first, and then the specific. The general is the context, the overall pattern of things. If you can't accept or believe or deal with this, then it's unlikely that you will accept the details of it. So the process just won't work.

For example, let's take the graphic case of the alcoholic and abusive father. You may react so much to the idea that you were abused that you can't get through it at all. This just didn't happen to you! But you may be able to look at the reality that you could not depend on your parents to take care of you, or that you didn't feel that you could trust them. As painful as that is, it is less agonizing to think about than a literal slap in the face. The context is also important, because what was actually most damaging to you in the long run was how your trust in relationships was ruined at such an early age. This is a lot in itself to grieve. When you have worked on that, then you might work up to looking at how out of control your father could be. Eventually, then, you can deal with how out of control he was with you.

Another way to manage the grieving process is to take in order the painful things that you have to work on, from the least painful to the most, and work on the smallest piece first. If something is too painful to tolerate at the moment, then dilute it till you can handle it. The idea is to do the work in such a way that you don't have to back away from it. Take your work one small step at a time. Trying to do it all at once can be a self-defeating proposition. You can keep yourself from doing the work by thinking that it's too big. Instead, imagine that you have a lake of pain from the past, and rather than opening the dam and poisoning the present with the flood, take a cup at a time and sprinkle it around and let it get absorbed and assimilated into the present.

It also helps to pace yourself enough so that you can, if you need to, deal with the pain within the confines of the therapy hour. In this way, you can contain the grief work and move on with your life without being deluged with your pain. People often have the impression that to do grief work properly, you have to feel it twenty-four hours a day. Clearly, that is not helpful.

There are other reasons that people back away from the pain. Often they feel that they won't be believed. In this case, too, it makes sense to test the waters as you deal with the pain. Rather than share your most secret and frightening pain first, start with a smaller piece to establish trust and safety.

Lastly, people sometimes resist doing the grief work because the suffering is the last piece that is helping them hang on to the old fantasy. If you are doing this, you may want to ask yourself if you are making suffering the theme of your life instead of dealing with it and moving through it.

Concrete Results

This grief work, and the work of learning to deal with real pain, has concrete payoffs in addition to lessening the bad feelings we carry around inside. Let's use Kathy again as an example. We'll look at the old way and then a new way of dealing with some familiar bad feelings.

Let's say that Kathy feels guilty and bad. In her old way of doing things, she doesn't question why she feels this way but, rather, assumes that she is bad and that she has something to feel guilty about, even if she can't name it specifically. When she feels this low, she just wants to make the feelings go away. She binges on food during the day, and this numbs her, but she still seems withdrawn and preoccupied. Her children don't know what's wrong, so they just try not to upset her; they feel confused and cut off.

After the kids go to bed, Kathy switches to alcohol. Three glasses of wine later, she is not only withdrawn and preoccupied, but also irritable. Her husband knows to avoid her when she's like this, because anything he might say is likely to upset her. She goes to bed alone, feeling her bad pain. She is convinced that her family has avoided her because she really is bad and undeserving of love. The whole pattern becomes a self-fulfilling prophecy.

But the new way to deal with her feelings is to question them and to try to understand them rather than to make assumptions about them. So, Kathy feels guilty and bad. Instead of believing it, she recognizes these feelings as old and familiar. She remembers what she has learned about them and how she blamed herself for what happened to her so that she could have a fantasy of a safe and loving childhood. She feels sad for a while, remembering what her childhood was actually like.

Then Kathy sticks with what she is feeling instead of denying it. She calls a friend, just to talk, just so she won't feel alone in her sadness. When her friend comments that she sounds upset, Kathy tells her the truth, that she's feeling sad, and she thanks her friend for being there.

When her kids come home, she may feel sad. But she can see, clearly, that they have a loving and safe home and that she has been a part of that. Her children will not suffer what she did. She listens to them talk about their day.

When her husband comes home, she tells him, too, that she's been feeling sad. She knows that the sadness is from the past, but she's feeling it today. Perhaps she has figured out what has triggered her sadness—perhaps an article in the newspaper about a child who was abused, or, perhaps, seeing a father and daughter getting along and remembering how she wished for such a relationship.

Although she may be a bit subdued and pensive, she doesn't feel that she's a bad person, and she hasn't made herself inaccessible by drinking and bingeing and withdrawing. This is the good pain that she is feeling, and it is pain that she can manage, that she can grieve, and that she can confront and not run away from, thus avoiding the isolation that running away leads to. Instead, she is present with her family; she is connected instead of disconnected. She appreciates her current reality, and she hasn't had to repeat the past.

This concrete kind of result is possible when you work on real, achievable goals in therapy. It makes life better! Therapy really does work if you use it to change how you deal with your past rather than to repeat it.

Women often get bogged down in therapy because it feels as if what we need and want is love and approval from a therapist. Rather than working on what will produce results, this kind of focus in therapy is one in which the relationship becomes a trap that prevents the real work from getting done. We want to look next at how to get out of that trap so that therapy becomes a place where we learn that things can be different, instead of a place where we prove to ourselves that they will always be the same.

— 8 —

Unlocking the
Relationship Trap

Carl was only the latest in a stream of disappointing relationships for Sharon. As she hung the phone with that old sinking feeling that this man would not be calling her again, she began the too familiar analysis of what had gone wrong.

She wondered if she had misinterpreted his seriousness about their relationship. Maybe she was at fault for not understanding that "serious," to him, meant only that he wanted more than a one-night stand. They had seemed to have so much in common. Of course, that was difficult for her to determine, because it always seemed to her that she liked just what each man liked when she was with him.

Maybe things had been too good, and that scared him. She could have been a little more distant, a little more mysterious. But Carl had seemed so down-to-earth, so straightforward.

Wasn't he the one who had asked her to spend Christmas vacation together? Of course, the vacation was on a deserted beach, *not* with his family. She should have known; she had blown it again. Wouldn't she ever learn?

Then she found herself reliving a few other disappointments from the past. Stu had seemed just fine. He was a darling with her family, had a great career, and would have made a wonderful father (she thought). Life would have been perfect with him. He had asked her to move in with him, and then he changed his mind at the last minute. Just cold feet, he told her. She couldn't understand why he should feel so scared when she had tried everything possible to make him feel comfortable with her. She could never understand how that relationship went from "let's live together" to "I don't think we should see each other anymore."

Stephen had been so exciting. He was romantic and highly intelligent, and took her to wonderful parties. She felt truly alive when she was with him, as if she could finally get in touch with the creative part of herself. When he looked into her eyes, she felt so close to him, so understood. She had never felt that way in her life. Yet, like the others, he didn't stick around.

Again and again she became involved with someone with whom the relationship seemed just perfect. She would finally be feeling really good about herself, and almost convinced that this was going to be the kind of life she wanted to live. Her self-esteem would be high, she would feel confident, desirable, happy. And then he would leave. And there she would be, in the pits again, wondering what was wrong with her, and yet resolving to get it right the next time.

So when Sharon went into therapy to understand why her relationships never worked, it seemed like a wise move. She picked a highly respected therapist, and she was determined to get to the bottom of her problem so that she could finally get the love she wanted and needed in a relationship.

Not knowing what to expect from therapy, she certainly didn't expect it to be so wonderful. Here was this man—solid, attractive, intelligent—who listened to her with his complete attention. She loved the feeling he gave her, and it was this feeling that she lived for. When she was in Len's presence, she felt the way she wanted to feel: safe, cared for, soothed.

Of course, she didn't have a clue about how this was going to make her life better, nor did she think it was a problem. As far as she was concerned, therapy was working because whereas she had been feeling depressed, lonely, and hopeless about relationships before she had started seeing Len, now she felt good again.

Completely unconsciously, at first, she began acting out with Len the same patterns she did with other men. She watched him for clues to what pleased him. She noticed that he paid very close attention when she cried about something that made her sad. When he was pleased, she was pleased. She loved the feeling of approval and validation she felt from this kind of attention, and she would automatically do what she could to get it.

Len liked her to talk about her dreams, too, it seemed, so she eagerly shared her dreams, perhaps even elaborating on them, just a little. She kept a journal and wrote in it frequently, noting her most interesting dreams and her deepest and most intimate thoughts. She thought about her therapy sessions much of the time and was happy that Len seemed pleased with her. And although she tried to ward off the thought because it made her anxious, she really hoped that she would become his favorite client, that he would look forward to seeing her more than anyone else. She also secretly entertained the thought that someday he would want to be her friend. Or even more.

Ironically, although she had gone to therapy to get help for herself, now Sharon wasn't thinking about herself at all. She thought only about Len and about how she could get him to like her and pay attention to her. It was predictable that this would happen, because Sharon never really thought of herself in any relationship except in terms of how she could please the other person. For many years finding love had been her goal in life, and she believed that being loved would solve her problems. Her whole focus in life was pleasing others so that she could get what she needed from them. If she could just find a way to be sure of that love, then she would be happy.

An Empty Space to Fill

Sharon came from an intact and loving family. Her father, Will, although very successful, was never a workaholic. He spent many evenings, long weekends, and vacations with his children. He loved going to their games and plays and praised them mightily for their accomplishments.

Sharon's mother, Rose, was equally committed to family life and her children. The daughter of wealthy socialite parents, she had never wanted for any material need. She had been a debutante and learned early in life how to run a successful fundraiser. Though she never supported herself after marriage, she had gone to a top women's college and was an accomplished musician.

Rose was a perfectionist. She was so bright and talented that she came to believe that she could accomplish anything she wanted. And one of the things that she needed to do perfectly was raising her children. Her children's accomplishments reflected on her, and she expected them to excel. They did; they were perfectly behaved, wonderful, and gratifying children. Their perfection, however, came with a high cost. They learned that they must earn the approval of the outside world. Appearances were vitally important; performance and production were rewarded. What was inside wasn't treated as important. And even though their parents actually loved them very much, they never felt loved for just being who they were; they learned, instead, that they earned love by doing.

As an adult, Sharon was paying for her mother's need for perfection and her father's enthusiasm for his children's accomplishments. She was a quick study, and as a child she had learned well that she was responsible, for her actions, for getting love and approval. And she did get love and approval for all of the wonderful things that she did. But she never learned what it felt like to be loved just for herself, without having to do anything.

As long as she was active and busy and doing something, she felt reasonably happy. Her failures tended to be devastating, but she was bright, like her mother, so she didn't have many failures. She had friendships that felt solid. She was a good friend to others, because she was always there, always came through when someone needed her.

In her quiet and solitary moments, she noticed that something was missing. She began to feel somewhat anxious, with her anxiety sometimes building to a panic. Who am I? she would wonder. Without outside verification as to her value and worth, she felt as if she had none. In order to escape this feeling, she went frantically from activity to activity, burying herself in busyness.

But relationships were her downfall. With her well-practiced style of performance, she tended to orchestrate her relationships. She had no sense that they would happen because of her or her inherent lovability. No, she had relationships because she worked on them. But since most people experience this sort of orchestration as stifling and intrusive manipulation, she kept losing people. Each time, she blamed herself, and each time she tried harder (which, of course, only made it worse). And each time she felt a deep, empty space inside of her that she desperately wanted to fill with love.

When she felt empty for reasons other than a lack of love, she could distract herself with some kind of activity or work. But when she felt empty because she was missing real emotional connections, the emptiness seemed unfillable and endless, and excruciatingly painful. The possibility that she would eventually find someone who could fill that space fueled her quest to find that person. She believed that the empty space must be filled by someone who would love her, and she believed that she was responsible for making that person love her. Each time she failed, she lost hope that she would ever get what she needed.

Therapy revived that hope. The comfort and understanding she got from her therapist were just what she had been starving for. Here was someone who truly cared. Here was the answer to all her years of unhappiness. She found herself feeling and behaving as if she were finally going to get what she had needed all of these years.

What Sharon never received from her otherwise stable and loving family was a sense of security that came from within. As an adult, she still strove to get what she had needed as a small child. A child will normally expect this need to be filled by a loving parent, and Sharon, the child part of her, looked to that loving parent in another form. Her therapist quickly ceased being who he was and assumed the role of the person who would fill up the empty space within her.

It Had to Be You

All of this hope, wish, and need gets transferred onto the therapist. *This* is where I will finally get what I need. *This* is the relationship that will finally fix my problems. *This* is the person who will do it. A real need and a real person get linked in a way that doesn't make strictly rational sense.

A therapist can help, to be sure, and Len, Sharon's therapist, is very capable of helping Sharon. As a person, he may be wonderful, loving, and understanding; as a therapist, he may provide a healthy and healing relationship. But if this relationship becomes an end in itself, rather than a tool for feeling better, Sharon has created for herself another relationship trap.

The advantage of the therapy relationship, clearly, is that this repetitive process can be brought into the open. Here, Sharon has the opportunity to discover something vitally important: that everything she has been doing to try to get what she wants is actually preventing her from achieving her goal.

Sharon has always believed that she must *work* to make people love her. Since she hasn't been able to feel lovable just for who she is, she puts tremendous effort into getting people to care for her. But this way of being in relationships is her own private reality, one not shared by others. In her mind, a bargain has been struck in which she will be loved in exchange for all that she tries to do for another. But nobody is on the other side of the bargain with Sharon. And, in actuality, people don't like all the fuss Sharon makes over them. They feel pressured, smothered, and uncomfortable, and they want to get away.

When she tries to involve Len in her usual one-sided relationship of need, he can help her see it. First of all, as a trained therapist, Len should be able to understand what Sharon is doing to him. He may feel smothered or pressured. Perhaps he notices some way in which she attaches importance to little things that he says or does. Or he may experience the same desire that others do in relationships with Sharon: to pull away. So he is aware that something is happening between him and Sharon that is the same as what happens between Sharon and other people. This is extraordinarily valuable information.

Of course, most of us don't want to hear this sort of valuable information. In an almost perverse sort of way, we go to therapy for feedback, but we don't want to hear the most important feedback. We prefer to hear something that makes us feel better for the moment. And we reject the information that will really help us achieve our goals.

We do lots of things to put off hearing painful feedback. We do the "Yes, but . . ." routine. "Yes, I hear what you're saying, but I didn't really mean it that way," or "That's not true in this case," or "I've thought of that before," or "I've already worked on that issue." Anything to avoid the painful truth. We continue to deny what we have always denied.

But our therapist is there to help, as kindly as possible, to break through that denial. Sharon doesn't want to hear that everything she has been doing to bring people closer has actually been pushing them away. Without learning this hard truth, however, she will continue to repeat her behavior and to disappoint herself.

Len, as a skilled therapist, isn't going to bombard her with feedback. But, for example, he may ask her why she thinks she's feeling better, and help her to question whether she is just covering up her pain with her good feelings about him. He may ask how she feels about him in general, or he may point out a specific instance when Sharon seems to be working to make him like her. Or he may stop Sharon when he feels like distancing himself from her and ask her what she is thinking and feeling at the time. All of these examples are ways in which he can begin to help Sharon look at what she actually does in relationships, because it is happening right in the room, in the present, between the two of them.

As this pattern gets looked at, Sharon may learn that her behavior is not working in relationships. Difficult as it will be to acknowledge that she's been putting out all this effort to no avail, acceptance is the only thing that's going to allow her to make another choice. What a gift and an opportunity it is to have someone trustworthy and understanding to point out where the real problems are. The tendency in therapy is to repeat the same old relationships; the opportunity and the challenge are to learn to do relationships differently. That opportunity and challenge are available to Sharon if she does the real work of therapy.

In her therapy relationship with Cindy, Pam does something very similar to what Sharon does. She doesn't replay her patterns in romantic relationships, as Sharon does. But she gets into the therapy relationship in a way that keeps her from using it productively as she unconsciously repeats an important pattern from her past.

Pam eventually loses sight of the "as if" quality of the therapy relationship. In other words, she stops feeling "as if" this relationship could make her feel better, or she stops feeling that Cindy seems to care about her "as if" she were actually her mother. Instead, Pam feels something more like "Cindy loves me the way my mother never did." When this shift occurs, the therapist's love becomes as important as the mother's love. Pam then yearns for and tries to earn her therapist's love as if the therapist were her mother, and feels in her relationship with her therapist exactly how she felt with her mother.

This is a dead end for therapy. Pam loses her original goals. She even loses herself, in a way, because she thinks only of her need for Cindy's love and approval. She's back to her original struggle as a child. Feeling unlovable, she must prove herself to be worthy of love. Getting that love from her therapist satisfies her for a while. But of course, this relief can only be temporary, because it isn't what she imagines that it is, and it doesn't really solve Pam's problem of unresolved loss from her childhood.

Pam needs to work with her grief that she didn't have a loving mother. That work is useful because it will allow her to see that it wasn't her defectiveness that caused her mother's behavior. Instead, Pam's mother had her own problems that prevented her from being able to be calm, accepting, and loving. Her life was unsatisfying before Pam came along. Having to care for an infant wiped out the last bit of hope that she would ever have something in life for herself, and she resented Pam for this. But even though she had legitimate reasons to be unhappy, they were reasons that prevented her from giving Pam what Pam needed.

Facing this reality and grieving her loss will give something back to Pam. She will be able to see that she is actually just fine as she is. She has nothing else she has to prove. But as long as she thinks her goal is to get her therapist to love her as her mother never did, she is not doing this work in therapy. Until she stops seeing her therapist as a mother substitute and does her grief work, therapy will never help her feel any better about herself.

Kathy's relationship trap was a bit different. Remember that Kathy thought of herself as the bad one in any setting or relationship. If there was a problem, it was her fault. She was, in essence, defective. Well, guess what that makes the therapist for Kathy? The good one, of course.

The good therapist becomes better and bettter as Kathy continues to see herself as bad. In fact, the therapist seems to be perfect. This is often called *idealization*, with the therapist embodying all of the most positive qualities possible. Of course this is unrealistic. It is also destructive to the client, who usually compares herself to the therapist and can feel only bad in comparison.

This dynamic was typical for Kathy. She was bad, and the other person was, therefore, good. Then she would feel criticized and disapproved of by this idealized, or good, person. Almost any feedback, no matter what its intention, felt like a criticism to Kathy. She would even get angry when her therapist said it seemed that she had to make herself bad. Instead of it feeling supportive, meaning that it was within Kathy's control to stop feeling that way, Kathy took it as criticism. All it meant to her was that her therapist thought she was manipulative!

Kathy's idealization of her therapist repeated another painful dynamic: she was used to getting a few crumbs of emotional support, and she believed that her therapist might give her a little something when she felt she was really bad. How could Kathy or anyone possibly feel good about someone for whom you needed to be bad and to feel bad in order to get anything? But that's all she ever expected: the wonderful and perfect therapist would give a little speck of support to Kathy, the poor, pathetic, and terribly bad person.

Kathy's idealization of her therapist also kept her hoping for something good to come her way in that relationship. Her goodness and worthiness, as we have heard in other examples, depended on her therapist's willingness to give it. Kathy had no control at all over what she got, but could only wait for the therapist to drop a few crumbs. We all come to resent someone on whom we are so dependent, and so Kathy was stuck in a relationship trap with her therapist, whom she both idealized and depended upon and yet, simultaneously resented.

The trap remains so for Kathy as long as she believes it. The escape is in challenging its reality.

Breaking the Rules and Unlocking the Relationship Trap

Each of us has a set of rules that we live by. We don't realize it because we take them for granted. But we learn them, over the years, and we believe that these rules of behavior are what make us lovable, successful, happy, whatever. Sometimes this turns out to be true. Usually, however, these rules that we learn in childhood get in our way later in life, as they do for Sharon, Pam, and Kathy.

There's an entire set of rules that women learn, not only in our early relationships, but also from society as a whole. Although men may also learn many of these rules, they are in general much more common and much more problematic for women. Women, as we elaborated in Chapter Five, get the message that we must be pleasant and helpful, that we must not focus too much on ourselves, and that we are responsible for smoothing and easing relationships. Chapter Five described the *relational self*, a sense of self defined within the context of relationships. If our success as individuals is determined by our success in relationships, it stands to reason that we work very hard on them. It is a cardinal rule that we must not offend, provoke, disappoint, or otherwise make another person uncomfortable.

This is not as altruistic as it may sound, as we are doing many things for many people in order to develop a better self. Since we believe that we are responsible for the success or failure of relationships, we need to be liked by everyone if we are to feel successful ourselves. We must work to figure out what everyone wants. In following these guidelines, we believe, mistakenly, that we can know and understand someone else without needing to check out our perceptions with the other person.

(Men's guidelines, of course, are different, and just as demanding. While we are expected to be pleasing, supportive, empathic, and "self-less," men are expected to be successful, brave and strong, and able to fix all problems as they arise. They have to be self-less in a different, and equally difficult, way. Dr. Joan Shapiro's book *Men: A Translation for Women* explains this well.)

Breaking the rules of expected behavior, which are both personal rules and society's rules, means taking some risks. For example, if we ask directly about someone's feelings or beliefs, we might make them uncomfortable. If we ask how they feel about us, we put them on the spot. If we ask them for what we actually want from them, they might say no and disappoint us, and if we tell them we are unhappy with how they are treating us, we might disappoint them.

Avoiding these confrontations is many women's objective in relationships. This avoidance restricts growth in most relationships. But in psychotherapy, it positively stifles it. Let's look at just how this happens.

We go into therapy to get help for ourselves. This requires us to focus inward and to concentrate on ourselves. But as women we have learned that to do this would be "selfish." We may go into therapy to get someone else to help us understand our feelings. But as women, one of our roles is to understand everyone else's feelings. We may go into therapy to get help with our relationships, but we women believe we are responsible for all of our relationships.

We are at cross-purposes. Our social roles demand that we get what we need for ourselves indirectly, by pleasing others first and then hoping that we get what we need in return. This is clearly an uncertain strategy for getting our needs met and an unfulfilling method for developing our selves. When women enter therapy, it is often because these methods aren't working, and they feel empty, angry, frustrated, uncertain, and unfulfilled. The choice of therapy is a good one. But, *in order for therapy to work, a woman has to learn to work for herself differently than she ever has before.* Everything our social role tells us to do as women is in conflict with what we must to do in therapy.

It makes sense that this conflict would result in stagnation in psychotherapy, because we as patients and the therapist are working in opposite directions. We will have to do pretty much everything differently in the therapy relationship than we have learned to do in relationships in general. And one of the main differences is that we must have an open dialogue about what is going on in relationships, rather than assuming we have the answers. We must also talk about what is happening in the therapy relationship if we want to avoid it becoming a trap.

This kind of honest talk involves risk. It requires women to break just about all of the important rules about what we are supposed to do in relationships. We must risk being wrong about what we understand; we must risk appearing selfish, because we are asking for something directly for ourselves. We must also risk disappointment. We might be disappointed if we don't get what we want. And we might disappoint the other person if we express dissatisfaction or complain.

Beyond shattering our beliefs about what we are supposed to do in relationships, talking about relationships shatters many of our fantasies about what we will get from someone else. But shattering fantasies is what the therapy is all about: the fantasies we've been discussing are the ones that hold us back and keep us stuck.

One common fantasy carried over from childhood, is that if someone really cares about us, that person will know what we need and give it to us. Having to ask for it ruins everything.

It's easy to take that attitude in therapy. "I shouldn't have to tell my therapist about this. He should know, that's his job." Well, not exactly. No one else can figure out what we want. Confronting a therapist with a complaint, or telling a therapist what we want, breaks through the fantasy that there is something magical about the therapist's ability to make us feel better.

Facing this particular reality involves grief. We go through life wishing that, somehow, our pain will go away. At the core of this chronic aching is the remnant of the childhood wish that someone (mommy or daddy) will make us feel better. We often go into therapy hoping the therapist will take the pain away, and it's crushing to find out that this isn't going to happen. No one can do it for us; we must do it ourselves.

Thinking about the therapist as a real and imperfect person who cannot work magic forces us to take responsibility for our own pain and our own work. We might think someone else can fix it for us. It's scary to think that fixing it is up to us. For so long, when we were small, we could not fix things ourselves. As adults we can—and *only* we can. That idea takes some getting used to.

It's normal to resist facing our fantasies, because if we begin to see them as fantasies, then we have to give them up. But when we do, there is hope that we can be ourselves, more authentically than ever before, with our real needs and problems, and still be cared for.

What to Do

To make your therapy work, you have to ask what you're afraid to ask and say what you usually don't say. To summarize what we have said in this chapter, women act out two relational patterns that make it difficult for us to say (and sometimes even to think) certain things. The first are efforts by women to fulfill our socially prescribed role to be helpful and empathic to others, to be the social grease of relationships, and not to think or act directly for the self. The second is the tendency to repeat relationships from the past in our present relationships. This is often tied to childhood fantasies that disguise reality, and so make it impossible to deal with what is true.

Here are some typical problems, some suggested questions to ask, and some directions to keep you out of the therapy relationship trap. These suggestions are not meant to be a script, but rather a guide and a way to make our points concrete. By writing them out, we also mean to show you that *you can ask these questions and you can say these things.*

We are also going to give some possible responses by the therapist. These are not answers that you should necessarily expect. They are, however, in the direction of what will probably happen, and are meant to help you see that what you might expect because of your old beliefs is not necessarily what you will get.

1. *Preoccupation with how the therapist feels*
"I don't know how to talk about myself without worrying about you."

If this is how you feel when you're with your therapist, then think about what happens in therapy if you are operating this way. While you're working at not offending your therapist, your therapist has access only to the pleasant and agreeable part of you. There's not much to work on given these circumstances.

Here's a possible example. You're eager to talk about how your kids are the most important things in your life, and you think your therapist doesn't have kids, and you want to know why. Do you just not talk about your kids and move on to the next topic? Do you talk about them anyway, hoping you're not hurting your therapist, and end up focusing on those feelings instead of what you originally wanted to deal with? That's the old way, the way we've been taught to behave, and much of it may be appropriate for other circumstances. But it's not going to provide much value in psychotherapy.

The alternative is to *talk about the feeling, the feeling in the present, in the therapy room.* "I'm uncomfortable talking about this because I think you don't have children, and I'm afraid you can't have any. How can I talk about how much I love my children when you're childless?"

It's the therapist's job to deal with her feelings and to help you with yours. So, she might respond, "I appreciate your concern for me. But we are here to deal with how *you* feel. I want you to try to do that and trust that I will be responsible for my own feelings." She might also add, "If I ever feel as if you're intentionally trying to hurt me, I'll tell you, of course. Otherwise, it's important that you try to say what you think and feel."

2. *Embarrassment and shame*

"I'm afraid if I tell you what I'm feeling, you won't like me."

This feeling must be present for anyone in therapy who is the slightest bit self-aware. We learn to hide our idiosyncrasies, our failures, our secret desires, because we have been ridiculed, ignored, or unsupported because of them for so often that we expect nothing else.

It's not uncommon to believe that we will be ridiculed because of a fantasy we ourselves have created to maintain a sense of control. In other words, we believe that we must be a certain way—good, thoughtful, selfless, brave—because we have created this false equation in our fantasy. "If I'm good enough or brave enough, then I will be loved." We go on believing our entire lives that we will be abandoned for our anger, fear, jealousy, or other negative feeling. What good will it do to act this way in therapy? What can we possibly say that is real about ourselves if we are so restricted?

Shame is a painful and powerful feeling. As women, we often feel ashamed without even knowing it—of our bodies, of our sexuality, of our supposed inferiority. Sometime before junior high school, most girls learn that who they really are is unacceptable and that they must become, instead, what society expects. From such early training, we learn to censor ourselves automatically.

Therapy must be different, or it will only be a repetition of the past instead of a way to an emotionally healthy future. The changes necessary to make therapy work take great courage, but risking your real self will be unbelievably liberating. Imagine getting not censure but interest, sympathy, and support when you reveal what you think is hateful about yourself. Never again can life possibly be the same.

You screw up your courage and say, for example (after a great deal of agonizing, perspiring, palpitating, and hand-wringing,) "This is incredibly hard for me to say, because I don't know how you'll react, but here goes. . . . My best friend is up for a promotion, and every time she has an opportunity I keep hoping she'll fail so that I'll be more successful than she is."

"How were you afraid I'd react?" the therapist might say, or perhaps, "It must have been very difficult, then, for you to tell me this." Notice that so far there is no judgment or criticism. The therapist doesn't have the same beliefs about you that you do. He is there to understand you, not to judge you. You will try to put the therapist in the role of judge or critic because that is what you expect; the therapist, however, will resist this role.

You might respond to your therapist by saying, "I want so much for you to like me, and now that I've told you this, I'm afraid you'll think I'm awful. You might never let on, but I'll think you're just being nice to me. After all, that's what I pay you for."

The therapist might answer: "Is it possible that those judgments you're placing on me might actually be yours? Because they're not mine. How do you feel about these wishes of yours?" The therapist is there to help you understand why you feel the way you do. And without the expected shaming response, you will have to explore other reasons for your feelings. Chances are, what you had been feeling so awful about for so many years will become something much more ordinary and manageable, or something that you can understand about yourself, with some empathy. In this particular case, you may discover how ignored you felt by your father in comparison to your talented older sister. Or you may find that you were taught that women can't get along with each other, that they're catty. Whatever you discover, once you bring it into the light, it will immediately lose a big part of its grip on you and allow you to work to release the rest.

If you believe that you must make your therapist love you, and that in order to do this you must not reveal negative things about yourself, you will likely get what you are used to in a relationship. In a way, you will likely prove to yourself what you had already believed about life and about relationships. But you won't gain knowledge, growth, or change, and you won't benefit very much from your therapy.

3. Preoccupation with the therapist, with his life, and with your relationship with him.

"I find myself thinking about you all the time. I often wonder what you're doing, and sometimes I wish I were a part of your family."

If you can't imagine yourself saying this, it's because these examples are given in order of difficulty, and we don't recommend that you start with this one. Discussing the two previous issues with your therapist can help you build trust. Talking about your feelings for your therapist requires that you trust him enough to make yourself vulnerable, and you should feel safe with your therapist so that you can benefit from this difficult dialogue.

If you find yourself in the situation in which you fantasize about your therapist often or wish to be a part of his life, you're very likely in the stage of idealizing your therapist. In one sense, you must idealize your therapist a little bit—after all, you do expect this person to be able to help you, and positive feelings for that person are appropriate. But if you idealize your therapist too much, you are in a transference trap.

In this kind of trap, you don't see your therapist for who he really is; instead, you have projected onto him qualities that actually come from inside of you. Your wish for your therapist to be able to love you perfectly or to accept you unconditionally comes from a childhood wish for perfect parental love. If you work to get this from your therapist, you will work forever and be forever frustrated, because you aren't working on something real—you're working on a fantasy.

If you stay in this position in which your therapist is wonderful and you, by contrast, are always found wanting, you are not going to solve your problems, heal your pain, or grieve your childhood loss or trauma. You will only repeat it. In other words, if you don't talk about your feelings, they will remain true for you no matter how skewed they are.

So, because you want to feel better, you take the risk and present your therapist with your emotional wish list. "And tell me more about how that would be if you lived with me," the therapist might say. There are many ways to go here. The therapist might say, "What do I have in my life that you don't have in yours? How do you know I have it?" The therapist will understand your feelings and empathize with you. (He may have struggled with similar feelings at some point in his own therapy!) Your therapist is working to help you be happy with your own life, and to free you from your sense that he is wonderful and that, by contrast, you are not.

The Acid Test

"What if my therapist can't answer these questions?" you might ask. Or, you wonder, "What if she gets angry?" These are important and difficult questions, but they cannot be answered without bringing them up with your therapist. You can imagine what you think her response will be. But if you base your behavior on her *imagined* response instead of her real response, you are, in effect, continuing to live your own private fantasy. This is likely to repeat the same kind of problem you have in other relationships: you think you know how the other person thinks or feels, or you have a wish about how the other person thinks or feels, neither of which may have anything to do with reality. A real relationship cannot stand a chance if it's subsumed in an imaginary relationship.

Let's say you ask the questions, and you're not sure whether the therapist's answers are helpful. Or, perhaps, no matter how hard you try you don't feel safe enough to ask the questions. You wonder whose problem this is—are you missing something here, or is your therapist not working effectively for you?

If, after a good try, you still feel confused and concerned that this therapist isn't able to help you, *seek a consultation from another therapist.* Of course, first you should discuss this with your current therapist. But if she is any good, she'll accept a consultation with someone else. The consultant will be asked to help sort out the dilemma—for example, is this a bad fit, is the therapist missing something important or responding inappropriately, or are you still in the midst of some old childhood pattern of disappointment with someone who's supposed to be there for you?

The results of this consultation can only help you, because you will learn something new about yourself to help move therapy along, or because you and your therapist will have a graceful way to say goodbye to each other. Again, we think it is worth the risk, because the payoff can only be positive.

Many of the steps we have recommended in this chapter demand that you care for yourself, think for yourself, and act for yourself in therapy. We have also talked about how difficult this is for women because we have learned not to live our own lives. So it is a great challenge to do this in therapy, as in life. It is also a great challenge to think about how to use therapy to live life for yourself, and that is what the next chapter is about.

— 9 —

Taking Control
of Your Own Life

It hung there in the closet, while she lay dying,
Millie's mother's red dress,
Like a gash in the row of dark old clothes
She had worn away her life in.

So goes the beginning of "Millie's Mother's Red Dress," an anonymous poem that illustrates painfully how women live their lives for other people. In the poem, as Millie's mother lies on her deathbed, she begs Millie not to do what she has done: live her life doing for and giving to other people, assuming that eventually she would do enough and give enough for the effort to be returned. Eventually, she assumed (though she never really thought about it) that it would be her turn. She lived her whole life without ever finding the chance to enjoy wearing her red dress; she died before she ever got to take her turn.

She did the right thing, though, according to all of the lessons that our culture teaches us. She thought of others instead of herself. We women learn to focus on the needs of others, and we learn that it is "selfish" to think of ourselves. We get the message that we ourselves are not valuable, but that the men in our lives are. We learn that we should be caring people, but that this caring does not extend equally to ourselves. By following the rules of socialization laid down for us, we live as if we could actually make everyone happy, and we twist ourselves into pretzels trying to do so. We learn that if we do all of these things for other people, as Millie's mother did, it will eventually be our turn: someone will give us what we need. None of this works, though. We have do get our turn if we don't learn to take it for ourselves. Doing for others will do you in!

All of these lessons that women learn have something in common: they teach us that, while we should be concerned for others, we should not be in charge of our own lives. In a way, being in charge of our own lives is not part of a woman's cultural job description.

When we go into therapy, we know that something has to change in our lives. Whether we are desperately depressed or just chronically unhappy, we know that our lives are not working out the way we're living them. But we don't think we're going to have to change the way we relate to others. Living for others gets us by, doesn't it? People seem to like us because we do things for them. How can we give *this* up? We may be miserable, but at least people like us!

Despite our beliefs about what makes us good people, all that we do in the name of helping others or giving to others is not what makes people like us. Most probably, they like us in spite of it, not because of it. All of our cultural beliefs have to be challenged in therapy. And if you don't believe it yet, start working on the idea that you can't make yourself happy by making others happy. The work of therapy isn't about how other people feel, but about how *you* feel.

Where Is the Real Control?

When Louise's husband of fifty-two years died, Louise was seventy-two. A healthy, active, and vivacious woman, she had to learn to live her life on her own—a new experience for her. For the first time in her life, she put gasoline in her own car and paid the household bills. Her husband had treated her as though she were incapable of doing these tasks and in need of his protection and oversight. Until he died, she never questioned his assumption that she could not do the basic things in life for herself. And when she found herself on her own, she was frightened, because she didn't know how she was going to get along. She had lived her life as if she could not function on her own, and was in constant need of her husband in order to manage. It didn't take more than a week of doing these things for the first time, however, for her to discover how capable she actually was.

A term used often in psychotherapy circles is *locus of control. Locus* means "location." The *locus of control* is the "location of control." When we use this term we are looking at the issue of where someone places the control in her life.

Is the control in your life outside of yourself? Are you dependent on the outcome of external events? Is your sense of yourself determined by what others think of you? Do you expect others to make important decisions for you? Do you act as if your life will go according to forces outside of your control? Clearly this is an *external* locus of control.

Or do you feel that you are responsible for your own life? Do you make important decisions yourself? Do you value and pay attention to your own feelings and thoughts? Do you expect that you are responsible for how you live your life? This is an *internal* locus of control.

Unfortunately, gender lines often determine where our locus of control exists, with men operating with an internal locus of control and women with an external locus of control. Clearly Louise had been operating without her own internal sense of control. Hers is a classic situation of getting stuck in a role because of cultural assumptions of what men and women are capable of and what men and women should do.

Without an internal sense of control, we have to manipulate the outside world to get what we want. If Louise wanted to have a vacation at the beach, she had to make her husband want one. Then he would make the decision. How exhausting, and how frustrating. It just isn't possible to always control other people in this way, but often, this is the only sense of control that we have as women.

This problem with control shows up often in therapy when a woman wants us to help her improve her marriage by getting her husband to be different. She can't do this, of course, because she cannot change another person, but only herself. But this radical shift of perspective requires women to focus in a totally different way. Instead of expecting other people, events, or situations to fix our lives, we have to look to ourselves to get what we want.

Now, this doesn't mean that we cannot have an effect on other people; in fact if we change, we can sometimes have a profound effect on the other person. We cannot make another person respond to us, but once we change ourselves we can often allow for other, and often richer possibilities in the relationship.

The task for women in therapy is to stop focusing on things on the outside and to start focusing on things on the inside. This also means that we have to stop thinking about how our behavior will make others change toward us, and instead concentrate on how our behavior will affect us, *ourselves*. If you think about it, women's preoccupation with how other people feel about them is another example of putting the locus of control outside of the self.

The theme of "If I'm good enough, then people will like me" turns out to be a double whammy for women. By early training, we learn that our work to make ourselves lovable and acceptable to others will make us liked by others. We also create a fantasy that if we could only be more lovable, then this would fix what was wrong with a frightening or confusing childhood world. Our childhood fantasies about what will make everything okay are just the same as the cultural requirements for women.

Although you've probably been operating on the principle that if you are good enough, things will work out well for you, we are suggesting that you consider that this principle is flawed. If you want things to be different, you must change this principle of doing for others, or focusing on the outside. If you want a positive result from therapy, you'll have to do your therapy differently than the way you've been running your life. (To be blunt, if the way you've been doing things was working all that well, you probably wouldn't be in therapy now.)

Helping Women, Angry Women

Most of the women who come to us for therapy are angry. They may not at first think of this as their problem. They most likely come complaining of chronic depression or other symptoms, such as anxiety or an eating disorder. They may complain of difficulties at work, or of being overwhelmed with family responsibilities, or of marital problems. What often emerges, however, is that they are angry, angry that they are constantly giving to others and getting little appreciation for all they are doing.

They're having problems with false control, as we addressed in Chapter Seven. They are wearing themselves out trying to make everything in their lives okay by making sure it's okay for everybody else. Then they blame those they are trying so hard to please for not giving them enough in return. They don't realize that no one made this bargain with them. They are operating on a set of false beliefs that almost all women have and adhere to strongly. "No, that's okay, I don't want any," we say. "No, no, you go ahead." This is our way of being in the world. But this behavior deprives us of inner strengths, and makes us angry.

Patty is a good example of how not focusing on the inner self can lead to anger. The most passive and "helpful" of three sisters, she is the one everyone turns to when Mom or Dad needs help.

It is as if her life is not very important, as if it's easy for her to drop everything to help her aging parents. She doesn't feel the right to say no, and she doesn't know why people keep turning to her. It all feels unfair. But she doesn't come out and say that these responsibilities need to be shared. She tries to appear somewhat pathetic and helpless, but no one seems to notice. She doesn't get help. She feels overburdened and angry, but she decides she must be bad or wrong, or else someone would notice that things are not okay for her. It's either that or her sisters simply don't care about her.

The cycle is familiar to her. The worse she feels, the less she feels she can ask for. Her needs are unmet. Then she feels deprived and resentful. Her demeanor begins to be rigid and even hostile, although inside there is a silent voice desperately screaming, "Please, isn't anybody going to help me?" Since the voice is silent, no help is forthcoming. Patty ends up bitter, cynical, critical, and very, very angry. It is not easy, then, to give her what she wants and needs.

When this outward expression of inner frustration is directed at a husband, the husband is not likely to respond with helpful support. Naturally feeling attacked, he protects himself, usually by withdrawing and hoping to avoid the problem. A less available husband is most likely a less helpful one, and so a vicious cycle is created. Women have to take care of themselves to stop this vicious cycle.

As an analogy to illustrate how important it is to take care of yourself in life, think of what you're told when you are about to take off in a plane. This is after your "seat belts are fastened, your tray tables are locked," and your "seatbacks are in their fully upright position." You are told that in the event there is a reduction in cabin pressure, oxygen masks will automatically drop from above your head. Now comes the important part. You are told that if you're with a small child or someone who is disabled, *you are to put on your own oxygen mask first, and then assist others.*

Now, in this context the message is quite obvious. If you're asphyxiated, you aren't going to be able to help someone else.

You will be most helpful only when you are adequately cared for yourself. We think that this analogy holds in life. You can't help people very much if you don't have what you need. If you are deprived, you'll be angry. If you are hungry, you won't have enough energy. If you're frustrated, you'll be impatient. But if you're satisfied, you will be able to be open, thoughtful, even generous.

To extend this point, let's think for a moment about how important it is to learn to take. We may think that taking can only be selfish. But doesn't it feel good when something we have to give to another person is graciously received? The same is true for those who want to give to us. When we refuse to take what is offered, we disappoint those who care about us. When there is an easy balance between what one person has to give and what another is able to take, the interaction is satisfying. When we reject what is offered or available to us, we don't help; instead, we disrupt a potential connection with another.

We do other things in the name of helping that actually do damage. One of these is to avoid telling people what is bothering us in a relationship. This is done, of course, to preserve the relationship, but it does nothing of the sort. It damages the relationship greatly, because there is a loss of openness and honesty that renders the relationship superficial and tense. If you wait long enough to tell someone what is bothering you, you may eventually get so angry that you end the relationship altogether.

Elaine and Janet, who have been friends since childhood, are a perfect example of this kind of behavior. After having children, they had trouble getting back in shape. They commiserated with each other for a few years before finally deciding to form a get-in-shape pact. They would exercise and diet together and help each other stay with the program.

Their plan worked for a while. Then things changed. Elaine made excellent progress, got close to her pre-pregnancy weight, and started to feel really good about herself. She began calling Janet frequently to remind her to keep to their workout schedule. But Janet didn't respond in the same way to the plan. She realized that she just didn't care that much if she was thin. She was struggling more to accept herself as she was. But she didn't know how to tell Elaine she wanted to quit; she was afraid that Elaine would be too disappointed. And the program was helping Elaine so much. So she started screening her calls on the answering machine, often not answering when Elaine called. She began not wanting to spend as much time with her old friend.

Finally, Janet was able to say cautiously that the plan didn't seem to be working for her. Elaine, thinking she was being a good friend, responded by trying harder to help Janet! And Janet, thinking that there was no way to tell Elaine that she didn't want to do what Elaine wanted her to do, felt trapped. One day, Elaine called to suggest an early morning jog. It was the last straw for Janet, who felt nagged to death. She blasted Elaine on the phone for pestering her so much. They haven't spoken in eight months!

Janet's mistake was in not being willing to take care of herself. By trying to spare Elaine's feelings about wanting to quit the program (because she thought it would hurt her friend), she ended up so angry that she destroyed the relationship. It also doesn't do any good to focus too much on what you think is best for someone else. Although Elaine was trying to help Janet, she did a poor job of paying attention to what Janet really needed. Sometimes, even though you're trying your hardest to help other people, what you're ready to give isn't what they want!

How Can Therapy Help?

Therapy can help with this problem in two ways. First, therapy can be a place where you can learn to confront an important person with issues that are hard to verbalize. Second, you can make it your goal in therapy to learn how to be more responsible for yourself and to think about what you want.

The first issue is basically what we discussed in Chapter Eight. Your individual therapist is there to engage with you and to stick with you even though she doesn't like everything that you say. As a simple example, let's say that your therapist is late for your appointment. Do you respond in the old ingrained way and act like nothing has happened, absorbing the stressful consequence of this delay in your schedule? Or do you tell your therapist that you don't like it that she's late? Obviously, we think that this is the place to break your self-imposed rules and to see what happens. This is a place where you can look at those rules, see whether you believe them, and whether they really work for you.

Although dealing with these issues in individual therapy is important and can be a transforming experience, group therapy can be even more powerful. In group therapy, many of the same issues come up, but they are even more real because other group members are just like you, struggling in their own ways. It's like a real-life laboratory. And you can't use the same rationalizations that you might use in individual therapy to fend off their questions. You can't say that other group members are "paid to like me," nor can you insist that they're just "saying that to make me feel better." If they do something that is hurtful or troubling, chances are you're going to feel about it exactly as you would in other compartments of your life. In this setting, you can explore the hurt, understand it, and learn to respond differently.

For example, let's say that something is really bothering you that you would like to talk about in group. Before you begin, you look around to see whether it's going to be okay to bring it up. "If nobody else has something pressing," you say, "there's something that's been bothering me for a while I'd like to talk about." There are nods of agreement, but then someone turns to another group member who had been very upset the week before and says, "First, I'd just like to know how Katie's doing. I've been worrying about you all week." Well, Katie still has a lot to talk about, and before you know it, group is over, and you haven't gotten to your issue. You're going to stew about it all week. You may feel angry or hurt. You may decide that your problems aren't really that significant after all, that you should be grateful for what you have, and that you shouldn't bring something up if it isn't a crisis. Being cut off as you were is going to be a real issue for you, probably an old issue, and you're going to have to struggle with how to deal with it. At some point, if you are committed to the group, you will. Perhaps with anger, perhaps with sadness, perhaps with frustration.

However you do it, this represents an opportunity to learn to do things differently. In fact, in our practices, if a client has to choose between individual and group psychotherapy, we often recommend group therapy as the therapy of choice.

Therapy can also help you learn how to be more responsible for the way you think and feel. In learning these new ways, you are very likely to need some concrete help, and you will need to take some specific actions to do things differently. Until you experience the positive results of living your life for yourself, you may continue to believe that to do so is a bad thing. Here are some specific steps you can take to become more responsible for your own well-being:

1. Think about what you want.

We've learned not to make simple decisions, like what movie to see or what restaurant to go to. What if our choice isn't someone else's? What if we pick the movie and it turns out to be lousy? Since we feel so responsible for how everybody else feels, we tend not to impose our preferences, because then we don't have to deal with the guilt if what we want doesn't please others. We also live without awareness of ourselves! So, start with making up your own mind.

After making up your own mind, the next step is to state your opinion. People will have different responses to what you say, and they will not always agree with you. But you have to assume that they can manage their own feelings about what you say. Practice letting them deal with their own feelings themselves.

These are important and often difficult tasks. State them as goals in your therapy. Ask for support. Make an agreement with your therapist that you will do them, and discuss the outcome in therapy. You didn't even think about what movie you wanted to see? Why not?

2. Take the space and the time to tune in to your inner self.

Wow, what a struggle this can be! Everything and anything will interfere with making ourselves a priority. And yet, without committing to making a space in our daily lives that is free from the requirement to think of others, we just won't do it.

You may need to meditate. You may need to designate a special chair in an uncluttered place where you sit with a cup of freshly made tea and think. Perhaps what works for you is sitting in a café, alone, with a journal in which to jot down notes. Perhaps you are fortunate enough to be able to go for a massage regularly. These are all ways to make space for yourself. What works for you will be uniquely yours; you must struggle to find it.

Once you have found the space, try not to use the time to think of tasks left undone, or niggling worries. If you find yourself drifting, that's okay. Let yourself go!

3. Learn to make commitments that are consistent with what you want for yourself.

How often do we say yes to a request without even taking a moment to think about whether or not we really want to do it? Build in some time between a request and your response. Don't make an immediate commitment. Explain that you need to think about what they would like from you before making a commitment. Then think about what you want. Do you have mixed feelings? Write down the pros and the cons. Treat yourself and what you do as valuable, and don't just give yourself away. Don't expect many hurrah's for your new behavior except perhaps from your therapist and friends and family who know the importance of your learning to live for yourself. The rest of the world may be disappointed. Let them deal with it; they'll be okay.

4. Do things that are fun.

This can be so difficult that women sometimes ask us to write it down on a prescription pad as a doctor's order! Having fun can be so far down on our list of priorities that we forget how to do it.

Many women will have to put serious thought into having fun. "Now, what was it I used to love so much?" You may find the clue to lightness of heart from something in your current life, or something way back in your childhood. Buy finger paints if you want to! Go roller skating. Turn on the stereo and dance around the house. Buy a joke book. Watch Comedy Central on TV. Plant a garden with flowers that are your favorite colors.

5. Think about what you would do if you had only six months to live.

Now, obviously, most of us can't drop everything and sail around the world. But you can think about how you would want to live your life if you had only a short time left. Would you look at the sky more? Would you spend more time with the people you love? Would you write that story? When you seek the essence of your life in its final moments, how do you want it to be? Put more of that in your life!

6. Ask yourself how you would be living if you were alone, and think about what would happen if you lived that way while you are married.

Often women who are married give up huge parts of them-selves because that seems to be a requirement. Chances are, most of what you want is going to enhance, rather than detract from, the relationship. Don't make assumptions about it. Question it, and bring it up as an issue in therapy. What are you afraid will happen if you are yourself within a relationship?

7. Go to some kind of gathering or activity that is for women only.

We have talked about how important women's therapy groups are. But other groups of women can meet many of the same needs as actual therapy groups. Be careful not to pick women's groups whose function is to serve others; that's obvi-ously not our focus here. But there are book clubs, study groups, support groups, and spiritual groups meeting to talk about com-mon issues. If you can't find one, form your own group where you can begin to express yourself honestly, listen to others with similar problems, and feel support for who you are.

8. Anytime you find yourself thinking, "I have to," or "I should," question that assumption.

Bring the hard questions, the big difficulties to your therapist. You're doing something new, and you're going to need support, feedback, suggestions, and sometimes a good push!

It takes courage to say what you want because you've been taught not to. You've been taught to please other people. You have to accept that not everyone is going to respond with applause when you start taking care of yourself. But that's okay. Everyone's entitled to his or her own response to you. Trying to control other's feelings steals your energy. You need to use more of it for yourself.

When we give up something because we think not doing so would be selfish, the outcome doesn't usually end up being so selfless. We actually end up making others pay for our sacrifice in some indirect way, either through anger and resentment or through sadness and martyrdom. We act out of our unconscious feelings and do something mean. How much better it would be to simply be clear about what we want and to try in reasonable ways to get it.

Giving Up the Fantasies

We've learned to operate in the world as if certain bargains have been made with us. Some of these bargains have to do with cultural expectations. One of them is that if we are "good women" we will be cared for, but we may have to give up our sense of self in order to be this good woman who is such a compliant helpmate. The bargain may not be such a good one.

Some of these bargains are part of our own personal childhood fantasies, the ones that were supposed to make everything okay. However, usually there is no one else keeping the other side of the bargain. We may believe that "If I'm nice, I'll get the love I want." Well, maybe, and maybe not. Maybe the other person has no love to give. And maybe your "nice" turns out to be not so nice, but is, instead, accompanied by the undercurrent of resentment, or even overt anger or fear, that goes with being deprived.

The point is that giving up control of your own life and putting your emotional well-being in the hands of another is unproductive at best, and at worst can condemn you to a life of disappointment and frustration.

But what do you do with everything you've learned about how to be? And if these bargains don't work, what will you put in their place? If you give up what you know, will you be left with nothing? The answer is no. But you do need to know what will be there instead. There is plenty of good stuff to replace what you're giving up.

In the final section of this book we present our chart, which we will serve as a guide to where you want to go. In this chart we will help you see what the future can promise you in place of what you have now. There is something richer and fuller for you if you take the risk to change.

— 10 —

The Chart

Now we want to present a powerful tool for achieving your positive goals. So far, we have been talking about facing painful realities, about moving away from destructive fantasies, and about making the changes you want to make. We have also talked about the natural resistance to facing those painful realities and about how easy it is to get sidetracked into dealing with unproductive issues in therapy.

This chart will help make therapy progress much more rapidly because it shows exactly what the work must be. But first, we will summarize briefly what happened to Kathy, because her story can serve as a model to show what the chart is and how it works.

Kathy found fault with *everything* about herself. She was convinced that her life and the lives of everyone around her would be better if only she were an entirely different person. She spent many years in therapy focusing on how bad she felt about herself, so it surprised her to learn that there was not much profit in dealing with all that pain. Focusing on herself as being at fault, and bad, was useless because she wasn't working on what was really wrong.

The reason for this, she learned, is that as real as her pain was to her, it was based on her beliefs about how things were, or, in other words, her childhood fantasy. (This was the fantasy that she had created to cover up a reality that she could not face.) Because she was living in a fantasy, and not reality, she made little progress: she wasn't dealing with anything real that could be changed.

From the fantasy, she got a sense of control, even though it was, in fact, a false sense of control. That feeling enabled her to feel safe, and the feeling of safety was both real and necessary to her survival. But it also kept her locked away from the truth.

In her fantasy, she had the ability to be good enough to make everything all right and to stop the abuse. Those efforts never worked, however, because the events as they played themselves out were not actually in her control, and so she considered her efforts ineffective.

As a result, she suffered from the *consequences* of believing that fantasy. If she never got the love she needed, she clearly wasn't good enough, smart enough—in essence, lovable enough. The ultimate consequence of believing the fantasy was to believe the worst about herself. She perpetually tried to find the love she didn't get as a child, love that she believed she didn't actually deserve!

Kathy needed help to see that it was her defensive fantasy (which she was keeping alive) and the consequences of that fantasy that kept her feeling so bad. Dealing with how bad she was, of course, would do no good, because it wasn't even true. What was true was what had happened to her in her childhood. And trying to get her therapist to love her would not heal anything, either. Only dealing with her own reality would be fruitful.

Reality in Black and White

Like Kathy, we all become experts at creating the fantasy that we think we need. Using denial, we live in these private fantasies, and, in a way, we live out our own personal delusions. In therapy, we may think and talk about our unhappiness, but just thinking and talking often allows this self-deception to continue. This is because if we don't address the purpose and the structure of our fantasies, we risk dealing with them as if they were reality. And dealing with fantasies as if they were reality is sure to perpetuate the status quo.

The technique that helped Kathy, and that can help you, is a simple chart that lays out each aspect of the problem in such a way that the relationships between the parts of the problem are easy to see. It shows you which of the parts is fantasy and which is reality; which is good pain (pain that is productive and useful to feel), and which is bad pain (pain that is wasted). By seeing this reality clearly, in black and white, you have the opportunity to understand just what you have been believing and how these beliefs are keeping you stuck.

In this chart, four main parts of the problem are laid out:

First, there are the *defensive fantasies*, the coping strategies that arose long ago to deal with issues from the past.

Next, there are all of the *painful symptoms*, very much in the present, that result from the fantasies.

Third, there is the *painful reality*, derived from the past, but felt in the present, that our fantasies were created to protect us from.

And, finally, there is the *positive reality*, in the present, that is available if we give up our childhood fantasies and grieve our painful childhood reality.

Seeing the fantasies in black and white, juxtaposed with their exorbitant price, makes them *undeniable*. Once they are there, "in your face," they are much, much more difficult to forget.

Creating this chart, in black and white, on paper, makes it possible to look concretely at:

1. fantasies;
2. the expensive price of these fantasies;
3. what the fantasies are covering up; and
4. the wonderful reward of finally saying goodbye to them.

Our chart enabled Kathy to see what her cover-up was, and how much more that cover-up was hurting than it was helping. It helped her to see what her reality was, that she could handle the pain of that reality, and that doing so would finally give her relief from her symptoms.

It can be confusing and complicated to keep all of these concepts in mind at once. The interrelationships of fantasies and realities, and of good pain and bad pain make sense one at a time, but can be difficult to see as a whole. That's what the chart is there to help with.

In order to illustrate this, first we will describe these issues in Kathy's case in the usual way, with words of explanation and analysis. After that, we will summarize all of it in a chart that, we believe, makes simple, clear sense out of all that analysis.

The Analysis

In Kathy's case there were several important fantasies. First of all, she thought she had a loving father. In fact, she thought of him as a wonderful, almost perfect father, and she never dwelled on any of his faults. It was as if he didn't have any. The truth was, her father sexually abused her. He was also a poor provider, and put his family through much turmoil due to his poor judgment and illegal activities.

Another of her fantasies was that she was basically an unpleasant person to be around, and that she would have been more cheerful if she'd only been a different kind of person. The truth was that she would feel depressed after her father abused her. She was told that she was a "downer" for everyone, which only increased her depression. But it wasn't a natural part of her personality; it was a normal reaction to trauma.

Kathy also believed that if she had been a better person and tried harder (a "good girl", if you will), she wouldn't have been abused, but would have been treated well and would have felt loved. In fact, it didn't matter how good she was. Her father's abuse had nothing to do with her, but only with his own poor self-control, low self-esteem, and selfishness. There certainly was nothing she could have done about that!

The cost Kathy pays for these fantasies is a slew of symptoms, most of which stem from her having bad feelings about herself. To look at just how this happens, we need to think about the concepts from Chapter Three, which explain our "love affair with fantasy."

Children lack the means to control many things in their lives. But, through fantasy, a child can create a temporary safety zone, a haven from helplessness, fear, and pain. The sense of safety that these false beliefs create allows a child to grow and develop. But the false beliefs about reality require false beliefs about her sense of herself as well, and these beliefs turn out to be destructive to the self and psychologically crippling. (As we do the chart, we will see that there are positive and negative aspects to having these fantasies. They work for the child for a time, but eventually, if she is to become a psychologically healthy adult, she must learn the truth.)

However, bad things happen despite these fantasies, these mechanisms of pseudocontrol. The child believes that her efforts will prevent the bad things from happening. If the bad things happen anyway, then she needs an explanation that will allow her self-deception to remain intact. Since her efforts inevitably fail, the explanation must be some form of "It must be my fault." This is how these defenses become crippling and destructive.

For example, "If I could just be good enough, Dad would stop being so critical," or "If I can just do enough things right, Mom won't be so sad all the time." Well, Dad continues being critical and abusive, so the child ends up concluding, "I must not be good enough." Since Mom is depressed all of the time, she thinks, "I must not be doing enough wonderful things." Self-blame, then, is the mental trick that maintains the fantasy.

This is an effective, but costly, trick. Remember that for a child, safety and a sense of control come first. Feeling helpless in a dangerous situation is intolerable. It is better to be a bad child in a safe world than a good child in an unsafe one.

How does Kathy's fantasy work? If her father was really good (as in her fantasy), yet he abused her, then she must be bad and deserving of that abuse. (That is, she wasn't really abused, only justly punished, and her father was not an abuser.) Blaming herself is the only explanation that makes sense if her father was in fact so wonderful. If she was just a downer all the time (as in her fantasy), then she wasn't having a normal, painful reaction to abuse. Instead, she was just a grump and no fun to have around. Again, it was her fault. (Better to be a safe grump than an unsafe cheerful child.) So she thought that if she could cheer up, the people around her would be satisfied. And since, in sum, no matter how hard she tried to be good, she was still treated badly, she concluded that she must not be good enough.

Now, what was Kathy's reality? Her father abused her and there was nothing she could do about it. Her family blamed her for the sad mood she created around her, and from this she learned to blame herself. Nobody helped this pained and terrified little girl.

What's so important about facing this reality? What's important about it is that by enduring the good pain, Kathy can see that her sadness isn't a character flaw but a normal reaction to abuse. She can stop thinking that she is no good because she isn't able to make her family happy and loving toward her. She can stop blaming herself for everything and stop feeling so helpless and powerless. She can begin to see who she really is: an adult woman with a real life to live and a family who loves her, who was once a little girl who was treated very badly.

Let's summarize the different pieces of Kathy's problem:

—Her father was abusive and her family was insensitive and blaming.
—Kathy thinks of her family as good and loving.
—Kathy holds herself responsible for all of the bad things that happened to her. By doing this, she gets a false

sense of control, as if she could have done something about what happened to her. As a result, she feels like a failure when nothing she does actually makes any difference. She ends up with poor self-esteem, a sense of hopelessness and powerlessness, and many other problems.

—Kathy avoids feeling the pain and sadness of her childhood, yet she experiences ongoing unhappiness in her present life.

—Kathy cannot appreciate herself for who she is because she is caught up in blaming herself. She has no energy left for creative and fulfilling activities.

—In her present relationships, Kathy feels inadequate and ashamed, just as she did in her childhood. Acting from this belief, her relationships are problematic.

Can you see how these fantasies, which originate as a creative way to save ourselves, translate into tremendous personal pain? It is actually the pain of self-blame, of guilt, of shame, of self-hatred, and of hopelessness that we feel. Amazingly, that pain helped us feel safe because it substituted for a different and more painful reality. Although safely out of the dangerous situation, we live life as if we are still in it. *But the biggest problem with this kind of pain is that, over time, it is much worse than the pain of the reality that it was designed to protect us from.* It never gets any better no matter how much we focus on it!

There are two reasons for this. The first is that we have to hold on to this kind of pain because it actually supports our fantasy. We say that we want to get rid of it (as Kathy wants to stop feeling that she isn't good enough), and we do work that we hope will get rid of it, and yet at the same time, we hang on to it tightly. We hang on because it has become our fantasy's vital support. So letting go of it also means losing the fantasy. For Kathy, it would mean (1) losing the fantasy that she could do something to make everything okay, (2) dealing with the reality that things weren't okay, and (3) accepting that there was, really, *nothing she could do about it.*

The second reason the pain never gets any better is that it isn't about what's real. That's why we call it bad pain, or "useless pain," or "wasted pain," because no matter how much you focus on it, and no matter how much you feel it, nothing will change and the pain will never get any better.

When you enter therapy, you will want to focus on the bad feelings that result from your fantasy. That's the pain you're used to feeling, and you really want to get rid of it. But your fantasy has been around for a long time; it has defended you and it has protected you. It will not go away easily, and maintaining it (your automatic habit) will prevent anything else from helping.

Let's say, for example, that one of the bad feelings you tend to have about yourself is that you're stupid. "I'm so dumb," is your habitual refrain. You are tired of it, and you want your therapist to help you with this feeling. Buy you are good at feeling stupid, and you are very persistent in your belief. Because part of your stated goal in therapy is to overcome this feeling, your therapist keeps trying to challenge that belief. So you and your therapist decide that you should get an IQ test to check out the reality. The result is in the above average range. For a moment, you realize that you are far from dumb. But a few days later you're complaining once again about being stupid. That's because the feeling has nothing to do with your actual IQ; it is a belief that in some way supports your fantasy.

Or, you might feel worthless. So you hope that you will feel better if you talk with your therapist about all of your accomplishments. But they don't feel real to you. For example, if you got an A in a graduate school class, you say it was because the teacher was an easy grader. If your friends gave you support during a difficult time, you conclude that it wasn't because they really cared about you but because they felt sorry for you. These examples illustrate that as long as the belief comes from the fantasy, no amount of dealing with current reality will help to change it.

The only thing that helps is dealing with the reality that you have been denying.

The Chart

It will be clear from this chart that living in either fantasy or reality has both positive and negative aspects. We can take all of the words that explain this and reduce them to something we can look at on a single page, something that helps distinguish fantasy from reality and that shows the positive and negative sides of both. No matter how hard you work on it, the pain of the fantasy never ends unless you deal with the pain of the reality. And many of the positive parts of yourself won't be available to you until you accept some painful truths. Using the chart, it should be clear that it's worth the work it takes to be in touch with reality.

Let's begin. This is a very simple chart with four quadrants:

The *left side* of the chart represents *fantasy*. It has a *positive* half (because those fantasies make us feel better and give us a sense of control) and a *negative* half (we have to sacrifice good feelings about ourselves in order to have good feelings about the fantasy).

The *right* side of the chart represents *reality*, which also has a *positive* half (all our good qualities and abilities, and the joys of life) and a *negative* half (we have to deal with some really painful and terribly disappointing things in order to have access to the good things).

A blank chart looks like this:

FANTASY positive	**REALITY** positive
negative (bad pain)	**negative (good pain)**

Now let's build Kathy's chart, piece by piece.

The positive aspect of Kathy's fantasy is that she gets to believe that her family was a loving and normal family, and that her father was good to her. In her fantasy, she gets to hope that if she can just be a better person, she will get the love that she deserves and needs. She is so used to making these little emotional bargains that she brings that process right into her therapy. She thinks that if her *therapist* loves her, she'll feel better! Kathy's upper left quadrant, then, looks something like this:

FANTASY positive	REALITY positive
My father was a good provider and an all-around good guy My family was a loving and normal family I was a grumpy, overly sensitive kid If I were a better person, they would love me If my therapist loves me, I'll feel better	
negative (bad pain)	**negative (good pain)**

These fantasies are positive because they helped Kathy get through her childhood. But, since she was actually treated badly by most of the people in her family, and since she thinks of them as blameless, she has to blame herself.

This self-blame creates all of the symptoms that Kathy suffers from. Because she thinks of her family as right, she feels wrong and like a failure most of the time, and she does all kinds of things to get rid of this feeling. Sometimes she drinks too much. Sometimes she obsesses about being thin, because this is something she can view as a success. (Of course, after depriving herself, she ends up bingeing, and feeling all of the bad feelings that go along with that behavior.) She feels depressed and hopeless about herself, and sometimes thinks that everyone would be better off without her.

This negative aspect of fantasy goes in the lower left part of the chart. For Kathy, it will look something like the chart on the next page.

These are the chronic symptoms that Kathy has—chronic and relentless because they support the fantasy. So as long as she maintains the fantasy, the symptoms will remain as well. They are required in order for the fantasy to maintain its power.

For years, Kathy has thought that these are the things that she must work on in therapy, and they are, therefore, the feelings and problems Kathy keeps trying to deal with, with minimal success. They are the bad pain, or the wasted pain, because they don't get any better, they just hang around, draining energy, resources, and hope.

FANTASY positive	**REALITY** positive
negative (bad pain)	**negative (good pain)**
(Price you pay for the fantasy) A bad person Stupid and incompetent Unlikable Angry Depressed Hopeless Drink too much Always worried about food and weight Lost Suicidal	

Now, let's look at the reality. It is very painful to be abused. And it is painful to get in touch with a troubled childhood. The painful reality of Kathy's life, as well as feelings Kathy has when she is in touch with this reality appear in the chart in the negative, lower right quadrant:

FANTASY positive	REALITY positive
negative (bad pain)	**negative (good pain)** Sad and angry about what really happened I was not safe in my family I was helpless and vulnerable I feel like the bottom is falling out and I'm losing my family Alone with the pain

Kathy feels sad and lonely when she is aware that she was unloved and uncared for as a child. Nobody wants this to be true for themselves; it causes pain that hurts horribly. And it can make you feel frightened, alone, and disconnected from everything you thought that you knew and were.

But it is vital to understand that this good pain will subside, that it *can be healed.* Kathy needs to focus her therapy on the bottom right of the chart. If she wants to make progress, feel better, and change, she needs to experience the real pain that has happened to her.

Sometimes we call good pain "grievable pain," because the grief process works on it to break it down. When you grieve something, you accept your pain over and over again, in many different ways. You don't expect to understand it all at once and then let it go. You know it will come up again and again. But with practice, you learn to tolerate the pain. And as you go through it, bit by bit, it lessens.

When you feel pain, when you grieve it and go through it, it begins to lose its grip on you. Unlike the bad pain, which is unrelenting, this pain will release you.

We've talked of the need to deal with reality, even if it is very painful, and now we are ready to look at the positive side of the reality chart. This positive reality quadrant shows the real benefits of going through the pain, and accepting and dealing with reality.

The advantage for Kathy of knowing her truth is that she doesn't have to blame herself for what happened to her. She didn't do it, she had no power to control or stop it, and she did not cause it. The imagined control is gone, but so is the sense of failure for not making it different and better. With that burden lifted, Kathy is freer to think of herself as she really is. The chart on the next page shows how we might describe Kathy's reality in its positive aspect:

FANTASY	REALITY
positive	**positive**
	Intelligent
	Creative
	Devoted parent
	Athletic
	A good writer
	Adorable
	Funny, likable
	Good at almost anything I try
negative (bad pain)	**negative (good pain)**

With this reality in mind, she can channel her energies differently. She can actually think about what she can do in the present and with her future, instead of being controlled by the events of the past. Facing the pain of the past reality has the reward of a real and satisfying life in the present.

Those are the four pieces of this simple chart. When we put them together, it looks like this:

FANTASY positive	REALITY positive
My father was a good provider and an all-around good guy My family was a loving and normal family I was a grumpy, overly sensitive kid If I were a better person, they would love me If my therapist loves me, I'll feel better	Intelligent Creative Devoted parent Athletic Good writer Adorable Funny, likable Good at almost anything I try
negative (bad pain)	**negative (good pain)**
I'm a bad person Depressed Angry Hopeless Drink too much Always worried about food and weight Stupid and incompetent Unlikable Lost Suicidal	Sad and angry about what really happened Not safe in my family I was helpless and vulnerable Feel like the bottom is falling out and I'm losing my family Alone with the pain

The chart shows very clearly that you can't have it both ways. You can have either the defensive fantasy and the negative consequences that go along with it, or you can have the reality along with both its painful parts and its wonderful advantages. But you can't have the benefits of the soothing childhood fantasy along with a full and satisfying life in the present.

By looking at the chart, the balance should be clear: it's better to deal with the good pain than the bad pain, and it's better to have the positive reality than to have the positive fantasy.

Trying to achieve emotional growth by dealing with the bottom left is a losing proposition. Facing the pain of the past reality is vital to a successful use of therapy. *Focusing on the pain caused by fantasies will get you nowhere.* The purpose of this chart is to help you break out of the repetitive pain you've lived with so long, and to give you motivation and courage to deal with the pain that *will* eventually help you get better.

The price of the fantasy is written out, right along with the fantasy itself. By looking at the chart, you can make a clearer, more informed choice of where you want to be—in fantasy or in reality. Most importantly, it helps you to see what the payoff will be if you have the courage to face reality.

But looking at someone else's chart is a superficial experience. Even if it begins to stir a feeling in you, it's very easy to dismiss that feeling. Someone else's problems, after all, are never as real as your own. To get a firm grasp of these ideas and to better understand how they can help you, you must make your own chart. We will now talk you through the process of making your own chart. We urge you to do this, and to do it in your own therapy if that is how it works best for you. But you have to *do* it, not just think about it, if it is going to help you to change your life and develop a sense of true empowerment.

— 11 —

Making Your Own Chart

Lila is a perfectionist. At least, that's what most of us would call her viewing her from the outside. She has a plan for everything, is always organized, and rarely seems to make mistakes. She does have trouble adapting when her plans have to change suddenly, and so she tries to take all factors into account so that everything will go according to plan.

She's one of those people you want to like, because you know that she has a good heart, and she is always trying to be helpful. But she is so persistently "helpful" that, eventually, you wish she would just help someone else. It's as if she believes there is only one right way of doing things. Sometimes, when you're with her for a while, you come away with the feeling that you're fairly incompetent, since you always seem to need her advice or help to do things properly.

Lila has never put this into words, but she acts from a belief that if she puts her mind to it and works hard enough, she ought to be able to make anything she does work out well. And so, when things turn out badly, Lila experiences this as a failure, and a very deep and personal one. This makes her life tense and painful, no matter how full of accomplishments it is.

Earlier, all of the things Lila did to "make everything work out" didn't actually accomplish that in the end. Lila's husband left her, and she felt her world had fallen apart. Lila was forced to look at her fantasies, and to examine things that otherwise might have gone unexamined for years. She had worked so hard at being perfect, and yet all that perfection didn't make her happy when her world turned upside down.

As you read this book, you may be like Lila, forced by life's circumstances to challenge your own belief systems. Although this can be a very painful process, it can also be a great opportunity for growth. What you were doing apparently didn't work; now you have the chance to find something that will.

Or, you may be more like Pam: chronically depressed and dissatisfied, with no clear cause for it, and nothing obvious to focus on that will bring relief. You churn around in your misery, and you can't get a foothold on what to do differently. This is a frustrating and often demoralizing position to be in. You need to find a way to turn chronic misery into a wake-up call. Maybe you're just tired of feeling so lifeless. Perhaps some part of you is trying to get your attention. The chart can be a way to get a fresh look at yourself.

Even though your own particular fantasy may not yet have proved to be a profound failure, chances are that it eventually will. Think of Lila, and pretend that you, too, have a concrete reason to want to rethink everything that you do and believe.

A sense of willingness to look at anything, and of openness to anything that may come up, is a key to using the chart technique successfully. Whatever you believe, be ready not to believe it anymore. We are going to ask you to look at what you have thought of as reality, and then recognize it to be your own, personal defensive fantasy. If your system has not already broken down, as Lila's has, assume that eventually it will. At that point you will have to find out what fantasies you have believed, and, if you want to change, you will have to give them up and stop denying your reality. Instead of waiting for your world to fall apart, you can learn to do it differently *now*.

Now it's time to fill in your own chart. We will give you specific questions to answer, and give Lila's answers as examples of how you might answer the questions. Her answers are there to help you come up with your own.

Tough Questions, Tough Answers

Each of the quadrants of this chart is difficult to complete in its own way. Therefore, different people will have more trouble with some parts than with others. We'll start with what tends to be the least difficult quadrant to complete (bad pain—lower left), and move toward the most difficult (good pain—bottom right). This seems to be the easiest way to learn exactly what to put in each quadrant of a chart. When you become more familiar with the process, a different order may make sense to you. That's fine, because it means you've made the technique your own.

The process is simple. Just answer some questions—some difficult questions.

Bad Pain—Lower Left

This is basically what you came to therapy for—these are the feelings you think you want to get rid of. They go in the lower left quadrant of the chart. The questions to ask yourself for this quadrant of the chart are:

1. What do you hate about yourself? What names do you call yourself? (Examples: stupid, fat, ugly, angry, unlovable.)

Lila would answer this question with "overweight" (she looked like a fashion model, but this section of the chart is not about reality), "inadequate, unintelligent, and unlovable." These negative messages were hovering around her all of the time, sometimes just out of earshot, sometimes very loud. None of the wonderful things she did ever seemed to change this negative sense she had of herself.

2. Describe the ways in which you feel bad, over and over again? Try to answer this question with feelings such as depressed, anxious, hopeless, helpless, or angry.

The feelings that plagued Lila were anxiety, depression, obsessional worry, and sometimes hopelessness. The standards she had set for herself were so high that she was in a constant panic that she might fail. Since she couldn't possibly meet her own high standards, she often felt hopeless that she would ever measure up and be the person she thought she should be.

3. Do you sometimes feel lost, confused, ambivalent, or vague?

Lila's intense, go-for-it style was present much of the time. But it was a defense, and sometimes, when she wasn't busy with a project, she would lose her sense of where she was going and find it difficult to focus. This is not surprising, since everything she did was designed to please other people, instead of coming from a more internal or personal need. When the hurry and flurry of activity stopped, she was lost. And her real feelings might come up—real feelings of pain. Confusion, vagueness, blankness are great ways to hide that pain.

4. Do you have any addictions? Examples are drugs, alcohol, food, work, spending money, exercise.

Lila had a problem with food. Always worried about her weight, so that she would be perfect, she tried to restrict her calories. But then she would feel deprived and break her diet, which would make her feel even worse about herself. She avoided alcohol because it made her fuzzy headed, and she had no interest in or source for illegal drugs. However, she had a longtime family physician who never hesitated to grant her requests over the years for various sleeping pills or tranquilizers. She kept a secret stash, which she depended on to keep her anxiety down and her productivity up.

5. Do you ever feel self-destructive or suicidal?

Perhaps the ultimate expression of self-hatred, suicidal feelings also come from terrible depression and an attendant sense of hopelessness.

Lila had never felt quite that desperate. Perhaps she was too busy to think of destroying herself. Or perhaps her particular style made suicide unlikely. But these suicidal feelings and impulses are common for many, many people.

So far, Lila's chart looks like this:

FANTASY positive	REALITY positive
negative (bad pain)	**negative (good pain)**
Overweight Inadequate Unintelligent Unlovable Anxious Depressed Obsessionally worried Hopeless Lost Addicted to food and tranquilizers	

Some of Lila's problems are very common for women, and as you read about her and how she made her chart, you may feel inclined to fill in the same answers. No matter how much you may have in common with her, however, you will benefit much more from working hard to insure that your own chart is uniquely yours. So before you go on to the next section, get a large piece of paper, make a blank chart, and try to answer all of these questions in the lower-left quadrant for yourself.

Positive Reality—Upper Right

This quadrant of the chart is what all of therapy is for—getting to experience *this*. When you are no longer bogged down by the old messages and chronic self-criticism, you are free to be yourself as you actually are—to be, to do, to create. Hopefully, you have had some positive experiences to draw on as you work on this part of the chart.

We should emphasize, however, that while it seems to be easy for most women to describe what they dislike about themselves, it can be equally difficult for them to describe what they *do* like about themselves. The questions to ask yourself for this quadrant are

1. What things do you like most about yourself?
Although a simple question, it is often a difficult one to answer. In fact, some women can't do it at all. In that case, the question can be rephrased: "What do your friends like about you?" When you're lacking in self-esteem or you're very depressed, it can be difficult to think of anything positive about yourself. But you have your good qualities, even if they're hidden from you.

Lila was aware enough to realize that she had some positive qualities. She thought that she was friendly, thoughtful (not necessarily a good thing in an 'indispensable' woman!), a good mother, and hardworking. Her friends might add "smart, pretty, and funny."

2. How do you feel when you are feeling good about yourself?

When things are going well, when you are operating on all cylinders, there's a positive, hopeful quality to life. When you are yourself, instead of trying to be who you think you're supposed to be, life just feels better.

Lila rarely felt a personal high, since her life was so full of doing what she thought was expected or required by others, but occasionally, especially when she was working on a creative project, she felt energetic, optimistic, and confident.

3. What special talents do you have?

These are concrete talents that, no matter how badly you are feeling about yourself, you might not be able to deny. But if you are feeling particularly down on yourself, ask a friend to help you with this. Things that fit here are "athletic," "artistic," or a "good musician."

Lila was actually quite artistic, and when she was arranging flowers or decorating or designing something, she was fully capable of enjoying herself. For better and for worse, she was also a great cook.

4. What do you enjoy?

Ask yourself what things you like to do, places you like to go, emotions you like to feel.

What kind of weather do you like? Do you like sunshine and flowers? Do you like long walks, intense bike rides, going to the movies in the afternoon, bubble baths, long browses at the bookstore, the smell of cinnamon? (Something to think of as you go along: it's good to use the pleasures of the upper right to rest from the pain in the lower right.

Remember to answer as many of these questions as you can for yourself. Lila's answers go in her chart like the one on the next page.

FANTASY positive	REALITY positive
	Friendly Thoughtful Hardworking A good mother Energetic Optimistic Confident Smart Pretty Funny Artistic A good cook
negative (bad pain)	**negative (good pain)**
Overweight Inadequate Unintelligent Unlovable Anxious Depressed Obsessionally worried Hopeless Lost Addicted to food and tranquilizers	

The Childhood Fantasy—Upper Left

This is the "positive" part of the fantasy—positive because it feels good to believe that everything is going to be okay. Listed here are the fantasies we create that turn a bad situation into a good one and make our daily experiences more pleasant. This becomes a more difficult quadrant to fill out than the two just completed, because to do so, you must recognize the lies that you have been telling yourself. It may be necessary to have someone help you.

You must ask yourself one main question to begin to fill out this quadrant, a question that has several types of answers: What lies did you tell yourself when you were growing up to help you feel better?

Since these are lies you told yourself, you needed to believe them, and so you think of them as the truth. You have to be willing to take a step back and use an objective eye to see that although you created them, they are not the truth. You may have to look at your present ideas about your history or your family or your parents in order to learn what you created in the past. A typical example may be, "I came from a perfect family or a normal family," when the truth is that plenty of things were not right and that they were not normal.

Answers to the question of the kinds of lies you told yourself tend to fall into three general categories.

1. Denying or minimizing the problem.

A problem is denied or minimized, such as by telling yourself, "My father drank, but it wasn't a problem." Other examples include "Yes, I was hit, but I always deserved it," or "They didn't want to hurt me, they were just overwhelmed." As you review your life or childhood, listen for a "but. . . ." It usually means you are using minimization or denial.

2. Making bargains with yourself in the present, just as you did in the past, as in "If I do ABC, then I will get XYZ."

In our valiant efforts to feel in control of an impossible situation, we strive to do all we can to change things. So for example, we end up believing, "If I am good enough, my parents will love me," or "If I don't make too much noise, my parents won't hit me." Or we might think, "If I can figure out how to be a better wife, our marital problems will go away."

3. Believing that things can still change.

People get *really* stuck here! The fantasies from the past continue, unchanged, into the present, as in "Someday my mother/father will give me the love that I need."

You will notice that all of these questions were directed to the family origin. We ask people to answer these questions first for their family of origin, then for their current life situation, and then for their therapy.

Lila's main fantasy clearly was "If I am good enough, then they will love me." Because of her parents' focus on performance and outcome, she learned to feel loved only for what she did, and she was terrified that if she failed at anything no one would love her. She also believed she had perfect parents, and that if she could have been less sensitive, she would have been happier.

As is often the case, Lila took this kind of bargaining right into her therapy. Automatically, she made it her goal to do therapy right, and she hoped she was her therapist's "best patient." (We know that this, too, is a common wish. Think about it, though. What does it really mean? Where does it come from? Getting well requires this kind of exploration. Don't take your impulses at face value.)

Lila also kept thinking that if she just lost ten pounds, her husband would come back! Lila's chart now looks like this:

FANTASY positive	REALITY positive

If I am good enough, then my
  parents will love me
I had perfect parents
Things would have been okay if I
  hadn't been so sensitive
If my therapist loves me, I'll
  feel better
If I lost ten pounds my husband
  would come back
	Thoughtful
	Friendly
	Hardworking
	A good mother
	Energetic
	Optimistic
	Confident
	Smart
	Pretty
	Funny
	Artistic
	A good cook

negative (bad pain)	**negative (good pain)**
Overweight Inadequate Unintelligent Unlovable Anxious Depressed Obsessionally worried Hopeless Lost Addicted to food and tranquilizers	

Good Pain—Bottom Right

Again, we call this pain "good", not because the pain feels good, but because some good will come of feeling it. This pain is about what is real, and it can be dealt with or grieved. To fill in this section, do the following:

1. Take each of the fantasies in the upper left quadrant and ask yourself, "What feels bad if this isn't true?"

You probably won't want to undo the fantasies in this way. The answers to this section are what you have been hiding from because you think that you cannot tolerate these feelings. But if you have come this far in your therapy or in working with this chart, you can probably do this part. By now, the truth is not that far away.

Lila's first fantasy was that if she was good enough, her parents would pay attention to her. She has to ask herself what feels bad about having been good and yet never getting her parents to love her any differently. What feels bad for Lila when she thinks about what is true is helplessness, sadness, loneliness, and anger. Her next fantasy is that she had perfect parents. So she has to ask herself what feels bad about realizing that they responded to what she did with excitement, pleasure, or gratification, and yet were never emotionally present for her.

To complicate Lila's problems, her younger brother was treated as more important than she was. More attention was paid to him, his bad behavior was excused, and there was more excitement about his future than about hers. What she felt was sadness and anger. She also fantasied that things would have been okay if she hadn't been so sensitive. When she realizes the truth that anyone would have had their feelings hurt if they had been treated as she was, she feels sad for the little girl she was. She recognizes that she was not overly sensitive, but that *things were bad*. And when she realizes that her therapist's love for her will not change her past, she gets in touch with her real pain and begins to accept the reality that someone's love won't make her change.

2. Ask yourself, "What do you know about your past and present that needs to be grieved?"

All reality that is uncomfortable should go in this quadrant. Doing grief work about anything frees you to move on in your life.

3. Also ask yourself, "What are the real things in life that are problematic or painful?"

Common examples here are loss of a loved one, loss of a job, illness, or some other physical problem.

As we are creating this chart for Lila, Lila has a good friend who is very ill with cancer. She also has the real problems of a divorce and broken family—moving, sharing children, cooperating with Ed, dealing with lawyers, etc. This is the real stuff she must deal with, and it is separate from her erroneous belief that she is worthless. (*That* feeling goes in the lower *left*.)

A common response from the women with whom we have worked is, "I hate it that I'm actually going to have to do this work!" That's a real feeling that comes with looking at the truth; it goes in the bottom right.

Writing down your answers helps in the process of making your truth into something real for you. Before we go on, do as much of this for yourself as you can.

Meanwhile, we are ready to fill in the last quadrant of Lila's chart. This last quadrant, in her completed chart, looks like this:

Lila's Chart

FANTASY positive	REALITY negative
If I am good enough, then my parents will love me I had perfect parents Things would have been okay if I hadn't been so sensitive If my therapist loves me, I'll feel better If I lost ten pounds, my husband would come back	Friendly Thoughtful Hardworking A good mother Energetic Optimistic Confident Smart Pretty Funny Artistic A good cook
negative (bad pain)	**negative (good pain)**
Overweight Inadequate Unintelligent Unlovable Anxious Depressed Obsessionally worried Hopeless Lost Addicted to tranquilizers	My parents couldn't love me for who I was I couldn't change them My parents had a limited ability to love I wasn't too sensitive, things were bad Sad, angry, lonely, helpless Good friend has cancer Problems with divorce

Now that you have worked with making your own chart along with Lila's, some observations will make more and more sense to you. We'll look at the different quadrants.

Lower left:

You're likely to find this part to be the easiest because you're used to criticizing and blaming yourself. It is the quadrant that seems the most real. But it is important to recognize that you have come to identify yourself with your pain. When you feel it, you think that it's caused by you and who you are. You aren't used to recognizing that it is part of your defense and that it comes from pain that you want to deny or avoid.

The lower left is a defense against the lower right. It is a very familiar place, a place to go to get away from what feels too uncomfortable. The real pain on the right side carries with it fear, risk, and anxiety, and there is a kind of automatic withdrawal away from it towards the left. The pain in the lower left is like an old bedroom slipper with a nail in it. You know how to walk like a contortionist to avoid the nail, and you just keep on doing it because you assume it is better than not being able to walk at all.

It is natural to want to get away from your chronic painful feelings, and there are chemical substances to relieve the pain. Unfortunately, this relief is only temporary, and the pain comes back, often worse, because it is accompanied by increased self-hatred for the bingeing, weight gain, or drug hangover involved. Alcohol and drug addictions are also chronic problems that go in this category.

Upper left:

Notice that often you act as if you could control uncontrollable things through your own efforts. You make bargains, the sort of *quid pro quo* of life. If you're thinner, funnier, more generous, more energetic, more whatever, then you'll get love, satisfaction, security. Because these bargains, even those in the present, still stem from old childhood fantasies, they tend to be unrealistic. The first half of the bargain doesn't actually relate to the second half. No wonder they don't work!

Bottom right:

There are countless types of pain and discomfort that get listed here. Life is unpredictable and difficult, but you have the ability to deal with these things. You have many inherent strengths. What made these problems seem unsurmountable was that as a child you were too little and too alone to deal with much of it. But when you look at it now you should be able to see that, piece by piece, you can manage it. You don't have to make it unreal anymore.

Upper right:

You should try to have fun with this section. This is your pay-off once the critic is gone. Over time, you can keep adding to it. As you let go of your fantasies, your reality becomes richer.

In addition, this section includes very simple things, like loving flowers, or taking a bubble bath, or watching a funny movie, or listening to soothing music. Sometimes these simple things are easy to access; they can give you relief from the pain in the bottom right, and can help you stay with reality.

Just a few more things: First, the lower left in Lila's chart is about as long as the upper right. The lower left is the way Lila is used to feeling. The upper right is the way she really is! It's easy to see that Lila would be much better off dealing with her reality instead of living in her fantasy, but what keeps Lila from doing it is the belief that she can't handle the sadness, anger, helplessness, and loneliness that led to her fantasy of a perfect family. *Only if she admits and deals with the fact that she did not have a perfect family can she enjoy herself.* We think it's worth it. What do you think?

Before we explain more about how to use the chart for greater self-awareness, we'll do Pam's chart for practice. See whether doing this second chart helps you fill in yours more accurately.

Pam feels "fat, ugly, incompetent, and unlovable." She suffers from chronic "depression and anxiety." She often feels "hopeless," as though she is just going through the motions in life "unfocused." Since she has been in therapy, she is no longer suicidal, but she still often feels that her "life is not worth living." She is bulimic, so she is "addicted to food." This all goes on the bottom left.

Pam is "warm, loving, thoughtful, intelligent, creative, ethical, and spiritual." She's bright and has a great sense of humor. She has a "beautiful singing voice" and, because of her volunteer work, is a big "contributor to the community." She is a "loyal friend." This all goes in the upper right.

She still believes "If I am good enough, my mother will love me." Where was Dad in all of this, we wonder? He doesn't get mentioned by her because she still believes that "he was just fine," even though he was passive and unavailable. She transfers this fantasy of wish-fulfillment into the present, and thinks that "if she can get her therapist to love her, she'll feel better." Her fantasies go in the upper left.

What does she feel when she faces her mother's inability to give her the kind of love she needed, and when she recognizes her father's incredible passivity? She feels "sad, angry, abandoned." She realizes that her "mother was inadequate as a mother," and that her "father let her down." When she recognizes that her therapist's loving her won't fix anything, she becomes frightened and confused. She thinks, "If that's how I thought I was going to get better, and that's not it, now I don't know what to do!" This all goes on the bottom right.

We put it all in the chart:

Pam's Chart

FANTASY positive	REALITY negative
If I am good enough, then my mother will love me My father was just fine If I can get my therapist to love me, I'll feel better	Warm Loving Thoughtful Intelligent Creative Spiritual Ethical Bright Sense of humor Loyal friend Beautiful singing voice Community contributor
negative (bad pain)	negative (good pain)
Fat Ugly Incompetent Unlovable Depressed Anxious Hopeless Unfocused Life not worth living Addicted to food	Mother was inadequate Father let me down Sad Angry Abandoned Uncertain about how to get well

You can see that Pam's view of herself—that she is incompetent, unlovable, etc.—doesn't fit well with the truth. Her beliefs about herself, and her conclusion that life is not worth living, are a result of her false beliefs that her mother will one day come around if she can only be the right kind of daughter, and that she will feel fine if she can get the people in her present life to love her in all the ways she thinks they should. These beliefs don't work, and so they aren't worth keeping. As her chart can show her, they aren't making her happy.

As we move to the next chapter, you can see how to use the chart to accomplish your real goals for growth and change.

— 12 —

Using the Chart:
Living on the Right Side
of Your Life

It was looking like one of those days, right from the very beginning. There was a power surge in the middle of the night, and your alarm clock didn't go off. So you're late for work *and* you didn't get to wash your hair, which always makes you feel unprofessional, even if you look just fine. While you're in a business meeting, someone sideswipes your car and, of course, leaves no note. (You carry a two-hundred-and-fifty-dollar deductible on your insurance.) Your sister-in-law calls to ask you to be a bridesmaid at her wedding (it's going to cost three hundred dollars just for the dress), and it's right in the middle of the time when you had hoped to take a long overdue trip to Mexico. And after work, you pick up your favorite silk blouse at the cleaners, only to discover that it is no longer a solid color!

How do you react when you have one of those days? Do you feel devastated, that you must deserve it, that you have all the bad luck? Or do you cope, reminding yourself that you have good days we well as bad ones, and you'll be able to laugh at this in a few days? (Especially if you get some sympathy from your husband—and maybe even a back rub.)

In other words, do you automatically get pulled back into the familiar painful and chronic feelings that result from those old childhood defenses and feel stuck there? Or can you let go of that old strategy and try something new that is based on the current realities of adult life? We can use the chart to understand why we might go one way or the other, and to give us some power to choose between them.

The Old Way

The more self-destructive way you might react to this particular day's set of disasters stems from the childhood fantasy of control. You blame yourself, or you attribute some broader significance to the events than they deserve and, as a result, you feel mistreated and angry: What makes me think I'm management material when I can't even take care of myself and get to work on time? Why aren't people more considerate of me? Surely they know I can't spend three hundred dollars on a dress I'm going to wear for four hours. Why don't I ever get a nice vacation? I should have a backup alarm clock. I shouldn't buy silk blouses. I should have parked my car in a lot.

The other way is to accept the disappointment and the losses, and to feel lousy about them. Chances are, given the cost of bodywork for your car and the wedding expenses, the trip to Mexico is off. It *was* a lousy day, as it often is when you get a late and anxious start. You don't feel very good about how you performed at work. You are going to have to find a replacement for that silk blouse, and the cleaner is not going to pay what it will cost to replace it. And although nobody but you noticed your hair, you felt uncomfortable all day.

When bad things happen to us, the first way of reacting is typical. It comes from that old childhood place where we imagine we have a kind of control that, in fact, we don't have. What goes along with that false sense of control is all of the responsibility we feel for the things that go wrong. In this state of mind, we believe that if bad things happened, we must have deserved them, or even caused them. If things went wrong, then we should have controlled them better.

The second way of reacting is to experience the loss and disappointment of an occasional lousy day. It assumes that we have some control over many things, but not absolute control over all the bad things that might happen to us. For example, everyone is late for work sometimes, and it's frustrating. Paying for bodywork is part of the price of driving a nice car. Bridesmaid's dresses tend to be a waste of money. Things just don't go the way we want.

We can locate the first way of reacting on the bottom left of our chart, and it represents the consequences of believing in the fantasy of control. We can locate the second way on the bottom right, and it represents the real pain and disappointment of life.

Without even knowing any of the specifics of this person's past, a simple version of this event, in chart form, would look something like the chart on the next page.

This example may seem trivial and mundane. But it is the kind of thing we all go through and about which we all have a choice. In other words, do we feel what is happening and deal with *it*? Or do we habitually turn it into something else, something more familiar but actually worse?

We hope that the better choice is obvious. But let's follow what happens to make sure it is clear. If you have chosen path one, you feel completely deflated by the time you get home. You feel like a failure. You were going to go to the gym after work and then have a nice dinner, but now you feel, "Why bother?" You get home, and feeling both tired and ravenous, start in on the M & M's. Then you *really* feel lousy. When your husband gets home, you grumble at him. You tell him it isn't his fault that you feel so bad, except that it *is* his sister who's making these demands on you. He tries telling you it's great that his sister feels so good about you that she wants you involved in her wedding, but by now you're deaf to anything positive. You settle in

FANTASY positive	REALITY positive
If I'm good, everything will work out right I can control what happens in life	Successful Competent Deserving as anyone else
negative (bad pain)	**negative (good pain)**
A failure Worthless Incompetent Undeserving Unlucky Ugly	Financial losses Disappointed about vacation plans Unpleasant day Bad hair day

for an uplifting and productive evening of situation comedies on television!

The next day, in your psychotherapy session, you spend forty-five minutes talking about how bad you feel about how fat you are, how you have no self-control, how discouraged you are that just when things start feeling better, you feel lousy again, and that maybe you should be on antidepressants after all. This is being stuck, isn't it? It's demoralizing and unproductive to you. It's also frustrating to your therapist, who has been over this with you countless times!

The New Way

But if you choose the second route, you do stop at the gym on the way home. Perhaps, since you've had such a bad day, you don't expect to enjoy yourself, but you push yourself through it because you know you'll feel better afterward. While running on the treadmill, you decide to live with the scratches on your car for a while, until you see how your budget looks. Your husband is already home when you get there. You tell him what an awful day it's been, and he suggests that you go out for dinner. On the way, you discuss his sister's wedding. He's excited for you, and he tells you that his sister called him as well, and that she told him that she's very happy you can participate. You're both sad about the timing because you wanted this Mexico trip very badly. But, over dinner, you find an alternative time to go. And if you are in therapy, you spend this week's session working on something productive, such as dealing with some unresolved feelings about your father's recent bout with cancer.

The first scenario, so painful and so pointless, is very familiar and common. But it's something that can be interrupted when we can see more clearly what we're doing. And this is one of the ways that using the chart can be very helpful. The chart can show you what kind of feelings you are having (that is, do they result from fantasy defenses, or real reactions to real things?), where they come from (that is, do they come from your childhood fantasies, or from the present?), and whether they are productive or destructive to you. Because, as we have said so many times, dealing with the pain from your childhood fantasies doesn't help you grow, but dealing with the pain from your reality does.

Using Your Own Chart

The first thing you must do to find empowerment and to live in reality rather than fantasy is make your own chart. (It just isn't going to work unless you know what goes in each space in *your* chart.) Then look in the bottom left quadrant. What are those recurring feelings that destroy your self-esteem, that leave you feeling worthless or hopeless, and that drain your energy? Let's list them on the chart:

FANTASY positive	REALITY positive
negative (bad pain)	negative (good pain)
Fat A failure Unimportant Undeserving Depressed Worthless Unlovable	

Okay, there they are, those feelings that come from various childhood fantasies. Let's say the fantasy is: "If I can be perfect, my father will notice me." (We can imagine this fantasy arising in a little girl whose father is too busy to pay attention to her, and who cares only about success and outstanding accomplishments. The little girl figures out a way to take control of a hopeless situation—hopeless because her father doesn't know how to relate to her as a little girl. So the fantasy keeps her hoping, but since her father never does respond, she ends up feeling like a failure, undeserving and worthless.) And let's give this hard-working girl a second fantasy: she believes that if she tries hard enough, everything will work out right. Now here is what we have in the upper-left quadrant:

FANTASY positive	REALITY positive
If I can be perfect, my father will notice me If I try hard enough, everything will work out right	
negative (bad pain)	**negative (good pain)**
Fat A failure Unimportant Undeserving Depressed Worthless Unlovable	

The Old Feelings Should Be a Signal to You

Once your fantasies are identified and in the correct quadrant, you can put them in their proper context. They are not about something real in the present you should be dealing with, but instead a response to, and a support of, some fantasy from the past. They probably helped you cope at one time, but they're no longer helpful; they only get you in trouble. So, whenever you have those feelings, you can now see them as a *signal* of something to be cautious of, rather than as the truth about you.

When you see them as a signal, those feelings can no longer plunge you into the abyss of hopelessness and despair; instead they prompt you to think to yourself, "Oh oh, something's happening, I'm on the bottom left. I'd better think about this."

It doesn't matter whether you're not sure you could handle what's happening differently. The first step is to interrupt the process of hanging out in that miserable old place of false fantasies and unreal control. You must *distrust* those feelings. *By definition, they are not about something that is real.* Once you admit that, you can begin to question them and pull away from them. And when you find yourself on the bottom left, you can ask yourself whether you've been having a fantasy and got disappointed when it wasn't true, or whether there is some other real pain that you are avoiding.

Chances are, something is bothering you *in reality*. But you are not used to feeling those real feelings. You've learned to blame yourself for anything bad, you are used to feeling like a failure, and you slip right back into that feeling instead of dealing with what's real. So when you notice you're on the bottom left, you must figure out what is happening in reality and work to deal with whatever that is. Moving over to the right side of the chart is what we like to call "living on the right side of your life." It is much better over there in the real world.

What happens if we add the reality to the chart? Well, on the negative side, there is disappointment and loss of some things you'd hope for in the present. There is financial hardship. And

there may be a family issue to deal with and discuss with your
husband because you're not sure how to take your sister-in-law's
easy acceptance of you—you're not used to that kind of family!
There is also the pain from the past of having been ignored by
your father—perhaps the pain of sadness and anger.

But to complete the chart, we add the positive side. You are
loved and accepted by your current family. You are good at
work. You do take good care of yourself (most of the time, that
is!). You are, actually, quite competent. So, we have the completed chart:

FANTASY positive	REALITY positive
If I can be perfect, then my father will notice me If I try hard enough, everything will work out right	Loved by family Good worker Take care of myself Competent
negative (bad pain)	**negative (good pain)**
Fat A failure Unimportant Undeserving Depressed Worthless Unlovable	Disappointment Financial loss Adaptation to new family Sadness Anger

Using this chart, we can look at what side gives you something worth working on. On the left side is what we have been calling "bad pain," because it is self-destructive and unproductive. This is the stuck place you may find yourself in in therapy. You wonder why you're dealing with the same feelings, over and over again. Your therapist finds she can't get you to focus on anything real, because you are so preoccupied with these bad feelings.

On the right side is the good pain. It is going to help you to deal with your financial losses. You can grieve your disappointment and come up with a plan to move forward. It will definitely help you to work to adapt to your new family. This is something you can talk about productively with your therapist. It may be new and unfamiliar territory to have a family that wants to embrace you readily and easily.

(When this happens, when we get something in the present that we needed in the past, it is most likely to reawaken feelings from childhood when we didn't get what we needed. Usually, when we finally get what we need, it makes the pain from the past even sharper for a time, because it's clearer how much better it would have been if we'd gotten it then when we most needed it. Sometimes this can feel as though we're backsliding, but we're not. When our circumstances change, we often have to revisit old issues and deal with them again from our new vantage point. But when we do this work, we both grieve that childhood pain again and then learn to live in a new way, and to move on.)

So looking at the chart, it's clear that the issues on the left are not issues that can be worked on. They are there only to keep the old fantasy going, and they stay the same in order to do that. But the productive work is on the right. The pain on the right is not wasted pain. It's good pain, the pain of real grief (which softens over time) and of movement and growth.

An Event in the Present Can Trigger Feelings From the Past

We just did a chart for someone (you, perhaps!) with a typical problem and a painful, but not traumatic, childhood. But how does this work for someone like Kathy, whose fantasies were necessary to keep her going in a very dangerous situation? Are her fantasies more difficult to give up? Does the chart work in the same way? Yes, basically, although the two left quadrants may be more difficult to let go of because the pain on the right may be more acutely painful at first. But the principles are exactly the same.

Kathy, if you remember, could be devastated by almost anything. She needed so much to believe her fantasy that she had to make herself bad or wrong at almost every turn. Here's an example from Kathy's past history:

Her daughter's teacher calls to set up a meeting to discuss the child's progress. Kathy immediately thinks the worst. Her daughter isn't doing well, she's a problem student. Kathy must be a bad mother and must be doing everything wrong. What must the teacher think of her? How can she go to this meeting alone? She drives herself crazy with worry. The night before the meeting she is irritable. She drinks too much to numb herself. Her husband can't calm her down.

She spends the entire time waiting for the meeting in her "bottom left." She feels that she is worthless, a failure, a bad mother; she's depressive and alcoholic. She does this to herself because she believes that she is basically a bad person, and that if she were good enough, she wouldn't have so many problems. This belief supports her fantasy that "If I am good enough, Daddy won't hurt me."

But in using this line of reasoning, since there's nothing she can actually do to keep Daddy from hurting her, she can only conclude that she isn't good enough, and so she lives her life with this belief. Here is the left side of her chart, and it shows where Kathy is, psychologically, as she waits for the meeting with her daughter's teacher:

FANTASY	**REALITY**
positive	**positive**
If I'm good enough, Daddy won't hurt me.	
negative (bad pain)	**negative (good pain)**
Worthless	
A failure	
A bad mother	
Depressed	
Abuses alcohol	

But Kathy is used to feeling this way, and she pulls herself together for the meeting. The teacher is very friendly and happy to meet Kathy. She says that Kathy's little girl is a lovely child and a good student, who obviously gets a lot of love, care, and attention at home. But the teacher is worried that she is so help-ful to other students that she may not be getting everything she needs for herself. Maybe they can work together to help this delightful little girl be a little more selfish! (It's not surprising that the daughter has modeled herself after her mother, and doesn't take much for herself.)

So the reality is that the problem is minor. Kathy's daughter does not have a serious problem at school. Kathy is not a bad mother—in fact, she is a loving and attentive mother. The teacher likes Kathy and looks forward to working with her. There is hardly a problem—at least *in the present.*

But Kathy has responded in the old way, as if she still needed to respond as she did as a child. (Remember the concept of repetition, from Chapter Seven?) As a child, Kathy learned to make herself bad in order to avoid the pain of the bad things that were done to her. If she had experienced that pain instead of the self-critical feelings, she would have faced the reality of being frightened, abandoned, angry, lonely, and sad. Those feelings from the past are real and need to be grieved; they go on the chart's bottom right quadrant. Until she does the work of dealing with these real feelings, she will keep repeating her old patterns from the past. And as long as she keeps going back to that old coping style, she is going back to the left side of her chart, the place where all that old and useless pain is.

But let's add the right side of the chart so that her chart, in sum, looks like the chart on the following page.

In this example, there is no new pain in the present for Kathy to deal with, but there is pain from her past that she has been afraid to face. If Kathy can grieve the pain from the past, she will no longer have to maintain the fantasies that protect her from that pain. And if she can give up the fantasies, she can stop paying for them with feeling constantly that she is such a failure and a bad person in the present.

FANTASY	REALITY
positive	**positive**
If I'm good enough, Daddy won't hurt me	Loving and attentive mother Likable Fun to work with
negative (bad pain)	**negative (good pain)**
Worthless A failure A bad mother Depressed Abuses alcohol	Frightened Abandoned Lonely Angry Sad

Getting Out of the Everyday Rut

In the example we have just described, we have a clear and defined situation that triggered the old feelings. We also had a quick reality check concerning what Kathy was worried about since she met with the teacher the next day. This makes it relatively easy to see that Kathy has reacted in an old way (as if she were in great danger) to a new (and safe) situation.

But Kathy often finds herself over in her bottom left without knowing how she got there. Nothing she can think of has triggered this reaction. It is just there. How does this happen, and how can we use the chart to help with everyday blues that seem to arrive out of nowhere?

This automatic shift to the left side happens because the pain from the past is unresolved. Kathy needs no specific incident to make her feel bad; she often feels bad because the pain from the past is still there. She can feel it anytime. And because she hasn't worked through it, the pain level remains high. Therefore, she still needs her old defensive fantasies, because she hasn't learned any other way to deal with her pain. And those old defensive fantasies are the ones she believes could have made things different if she hadn't been such a failure, so basically bad, so at fault. She hangs out in her bottom left most of the time because she hasn't dealt with the real trauma from her past.

When Kathy goes to therapy to talk about how incompetent, worthless, and depressed she is, obviously she can't get any better. That is how she got stuck in therapy for so long. Once she is ready to go into therapy and grieve her past, however, she can learn to cope with her pain in a new way. Each time she manages to tolerate her pain and not run away from it, she can avoid the trap of her old defense. She can be her real self.

This most likely happens to you, too. You have unresolved pain that you haven't learned to deal with. Each time that pain bubbles up, close to consciousness, your defenses come into play. The old fantasies are mobilized, along with their old consequences. All of a sudden, without knowing how or why, you feel lousy again. You overeat, you pick a fight with someone you feel hasn't cared for you. Then you feel really bad, and you actually have reason to, because now you *have* done something you can judge harshly.

But you have done these self-destructive things or felt these old lousy feelings because you haven't yet finished the work of dealing with your particular pain. This is the work of therapy. Doing this work is what will allow you to progress toward your goals.

It will take focus and concentration to do this work. It has been demanding for Kathy, and it will be for you as well. Knowing what to focus on is the necessary first step. But doing the work takes effort and discipline. It is so easy to slide back into old familiar patterns, and so difficult to make yourself face real pain. Our point in showing you how to use the chart is to make it clear that this work is doable, and worth doing.

Using the Chart Every Day

You can use this chart every day to find solutions to painful dilemmas, stop self-destructive behaviors, and get out of places that feel stuck. Your ordinary, familiar patterns and experiences can be plotted on the chart. Then you can figure out much more easily and productively what choices to make and which way to go. You don't have to do a complete chart each time something comes up for you. You can focus on the most relevant issue. Here are some specific hints about how to think about the chart.

Upper left:

When you are in the upper left, it feels exciting and hopeful. You get charged up, and you're glad to have that kind of positive feeling again. You know that you're in the upper left when you have thoughts like, "This thing will fix my life," or "This person will make me happy," or, "This is going to be the best ever."

There is a fantasy quality to this kind of excitement. Even though nobody except yourself can make your life work for you, the fantasy side seduces you with this feeling of "Aha! This is it! He's finally going to love me! Life's finally going to be the greatest!" Can you hear how fantastic all of that is? Of course, when you yourself are living the fantasy, you firmly believe in its reality. But when you realize that no one thing is going to be that perfect, you have a good idea you're in the fantasy quadrant.

The problem with this kind of excitement is that you will always pay for it with the bad pain from the bottom left. It's probably easiest to relate this to exciting but failed love affairs, the kind that Sharon always had. Again and again she would get swept off her feet by the man of her dreams. Then she'd wake up and find him gone, or important parts of herself gone. Maybe he literally took her money, but more often he took her trust. She thought he was going to stay with her and fix her life; she let herself believe that this man's loving her would fix her. Of course she didn't change, of course he left, and of course she crashed right down to the bottom left, right into her low self-esteem, depression, and hopelessness, as well as her overdrinking and chocolate bingeing.

That upper left is so enticing, though. It can feel so much more exciting than the upper right. It's a very compelling feeling, much more so than the nice feeling on the upper right. The upper right can range anywhere from pleasant to soul satisfying. But often it is just good and pleasant—not as enticing. But there is no price to pay for feeling the reality high once you have been willing to deal with your real pain.

Lower left:

The lower left feels like the most real thing about you, and yet, as you've learned, it isn't real at all, but only a defense against the real pain. This bad pain feels so familiar. You know all about it. When you start feeling it, you know where you're likely to end up. It's like going down a drain. You're pulled down a slippery slope right to the bottom.

Over time, a graph of the bad pain looks like this:

pain

time

You can see how it seems to change, seems to get better, but over time, it is actually very constant. It stays around forever, or in other words, as long as you need it as a defense. You will not change it by working on it in therapy.

This pain works perfectly for you as a defense. It will *never* go away unless you decide to give up the defense and look at the reality.

If you feel the bad pain, you can ask yourself: "Have I had a fantasy, and now I'm paying for it?" You may be able to shift yourself out of the pain on the bottom left by acknowledging the fantasy. The lower left isn't necessary if you move away from the upper left.

You can also ask yourself, "Did I feel some real pain that scared me, and did I run away from it to the familiar pain on the left?" The old pain may be bad, but it's familiar, and you're used to coping with it. But if it turns out that you were about to do some real grieving when you ended up back in the old place, you have the opportunity to return to where you were and work on your empowerment.

Lower right:

This kind of pain causes great anxiety and discomfort. It may be about something that we don't want to know or don't want to be true. It is very easy to back away from it. But the good thing about this pain, the thing to remember when you feel it, is that it's grievable. That means it will change over time. Its graph looks like this:

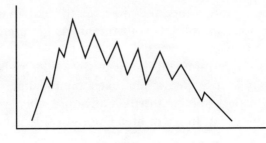

As you can see, the time you spend dealing with it will pay off. But recall what we have said about grief work: you must pace yourself. Do a little at a time. If a pain is too big, take a smaller piece of it or dilute it. In fact, one helpful way to work with this is to list your real pain in the bottom right from most bearable to most painful, and begin with what hurts the least.

For example, if the problem is that your father was violent, frightening, and physically abusive, but you can't stand to look at that truth, then try working on the fact that he came from an abusive family and didn't learn good parenting skills. Do you see how that is part of the same truth, but a piece that is more tolerable? Later, you can move on to the fact that your home wasn't a safe place for you. Only after you have managed to deal with that can you move on to "My father hurt me."

The point of all of this, of making therapy work, is that therapy is supposed to make your life better now, in the present. So it is important to grieve in a way that doesn't overwhelm you. Do a little bit at a time, with a lot of rest in the upper right. (See Chapter Seven, Nine, and the next and final chapter for more details on how to do that.)

Upper right:

Resting in the upper right is an important part of the work. Doing those things that feel good to you will allow the rest of the work to continue. But you may find yourself resisting this soothing, pleasant, safe place. If you have felt bad about yourself for a long time, the good feelings in the upper right may feel odd, frightening, or unfamiliar. Your natural tendency will be to leave and find something over on the left that is familiar, no matter how painful. Use your therapy to get used to being happy and liking yourself.

The more time you spend in the upper right, the more you will be able to enjoy it. The excitement-danger combination of the left side won't be worth it anymore when you can honestly enjoy the good things in life. The right side is not as exciting as the left side because there is no danger involved. But it is very exciting—and healthy—to have more and more of what is real. Eventually, the left side will lose its appeal. Partake all you can of the right side. It is a great place to be. Enjoy it. You deserve it. We all do.

It should be obvious that we believe psychotherapy can be immensely helpful. However, its also easy to get stuck in psychotherapy or sidetracked. We are confident that this book and this chart will make it easier to stay unstuck and to work through false fantasies and false controls. The last chapter is our outline to help you use all the pieces we've explained so that you can begin living on the right side of your life!

— 13 —

Putting It All Together:
A Practical Plan

Through reading this book, some of you will have been able to pinpoint where you are stalled in your work and are now ready to move forward. But if you don't know exactly what's wrong, it can be difficult to figure out where to start. Is the problem how you're working with your therapist? Is the problem that you're not working on the right thing? If you're not in therapy, should you be? Is it time to get out of therapy? Are you working in therapy but ignoring the rest of your life? Let's try, in this last chapter, to answer these questions and more, and present a very specific plan for figuring out what is wrong and what to do about it. Following is an outline of a path of decision-making, step by step.

I. Identify what is wrong.

   A. Do you have chronic bad feelings?
   This is the relentless stuff, the feelings that you are sick and tired of, or that really interfere with your life. Perhaps you suffer from chronic anxiety or a persistent, low-level depression. These feelings may be uncomfortable, and may interfere with your enjoyment of *your* life and with your productivity. Or they

may be severe enough to limit you. Maybe you don't go places you'd like to go because you get too nervous when you're around a lot of people, so it rarely seems worth the effort. Or maybe you feel so unmotivated that you just never get around to doing anything.

Maybe you have a rash of symptoms—insomnia, overeating, a run-down feeling, chronic colds. Maybe your problem is low self-esteem, out-of-control anger, indecisiveness, or the bad habit of letting people take advantage of you and then resenting them for it.

It is important for you to make the distinction between how much of this is internal (simply part of your biological makeup) and how much is more dynamic (in other words, the way you've learned to deal with things). This can be a difficult distinction to make. Sometimes people get so used to a chronic depression that they think of themselves as just basically boring or limited in their capacity to enjoy life and don't search out the causes for this.

If you have always felt depressed at some level, you deserve a psychiatric evaluation. It is possible that you are suffering from a kind of chronic depression that can be treated very effectively with medication. If you have been beating your head against the wall because you always feel blue no matter how hard you try to help yourself, you may benefit greatly from medical attention.

Even if your condition can be treated with medication, that may be only part of the picture. Because if you're suffering from depression, the other possibility is that you are stuck in the lower left part of your chart, producing chronic bad feelings of depression, lack of motivation, lack of focus, and hopelessness. Although this condition may have turned into a biologically treatable depression, it could have started from your need to defend yourself against some childhood pain with the technique of denial. Your chronic symptoms may be those of fantasies that have become too expensive to the self. In this case, you could need some serious therapy. If you don't get into therapy, you will still need to find a way to work through the long-standing issues that you have been denying.

If you have already done some serious work in therapy, and you still feel depressed, you are most likely stuck. The plan for this will be in section V of this outline.

B. Are you in a crisis?

You must ask yourself why this is a crisis for you, if it is. Is this something that other people seem to handle but that has knocked you over? Or is this something that would make anyone upset? Do you find yourself living life from crisis to crisis?

If this is, in fact, a real crisis, then you must *get support* and aid for yourself. Do what you need to do to solve your real problems and get all of the assistance you can to help you through the difficulties.

If this is a created crisis, and you are feeling that things are worse than they really are, you're probably in the bottom left of your chart, and experiencing the panic of crisis is one of the consequences of your self-blame. Maybe you have the fantasy that you can fix anything, and so when things go wrong, you panic because you believe you can make it all better. Maybe you feel so bad about yourself all of the time that you experience most of life as a crisis. You need help, probably therapy, to get to what your real pain is and grieve it.

C. Do you have a problem that you can't seem to solve?

Is this a kind of problem that you tend to have regularly? If this is an old familiar rotten feeling, you're living over in the bottom left. You need *to work to get over to the other side of your life.* This is the bad pain that you're feeling, the kind you're familiar with, even though you don't particularly like it.

Is this a form of resistance to change? Are you stuck with this problem because getting through it means getting to a new place that you don't feel ready for? This could be another form of defense, and one that needs therapy to help you break it. Or it could be cold feet about doing something different. Supportive friends in small groups can often help you through this without actual therapy. Let them be your cheering section as you try something new in life. They'll be happy to do it. And you'll inspire them to make changes of their own!

Is this a real problem? Are you having difficulty getting through this because anybody would? Just as in a real crisis, here is where you need to access real-life help. You may need to face that you are unable to do this with your current resources, and your job is therefore to gather some additional resources.

II. Learn to ask for help.

A. Is asking for help difficult for you?

Asking for help can be very difficult for women. We know how to complain, but not how to actually take what we might need. Since we're not supposed to "take," sometimes all that we seem to be left with is a helpless, victimized stance. We feel bad, we hope someone will help, but we don't really believe they will. The complaints are ineffective, and they become repetitive.

It can be a real relief to those around us when we just *ask for what we need* and take it. They are tired of being around us when we feel so disappointed.

B. Can you get other kinds of help besides therapy?

Obviously, we think that therapy is wonderful help. But it is only a part of life, and a temporary one. There are many other solid kinds of help.

Friends love to feel helpful. Yet they don't want to do it exclusively. But when we are able to help someone, we feel useful and connected. Do your friends a favor: *let them do what they can.*

You have to learn how to use your spouse appropriately. Remember, your spouse isn't there to make up for the love you didn't have as a child. He or she is there to be your companion, lover, partner, and helper through your old pain. If you don't project all of your old stuff onto your spouse or expect him to be the father you never had, you can *help show him what you really need.* Perhaps it's a sympathetic ear. Perhaps it's moral support. Perhaps you just want him to cook dinner for you sometimes. He can be your greatest ally.

Getting care and attention can do wonders for you: it can give you extra energy, a sense of peace and well-being, and a more positive outlook. Any problem is easier to solve when you feel soothed and replenished. Getting a massage, getting a facial, taking a bubble bath, sitting with a cup of tea—all of these can provide a sense of having enough.

If you're going to tackle anything big, you have to be ready for it. If you want to face your underlying fears, get through something you've been avoiding, and get healthy once and for all, you have to be strong. This means having a healthy diet (that is, healthy food, not depriving yourself of food, as the word "diet" has come to mean for so many women), getting plenty of sleep and exercise, and using meditation or some other stress-maintenance technique. Set the stage to get the most done by making sure that you have all of the basics.

III. Know when to seek therapy.

A. Do the extent and disruptiveness of your symptoms get in the way?

If they do, that's a pretty good sign that whatever you're doing isn't working and you need some help. Does your eating disorder flare up only when you have a fight with your boss, or does any conflict set you off? Do you get anxious when you have to speak in front of a large group, or does your anxiety make you miserable when you do anything new? If your symptoms are interfering with your life in a major way, it's probably time for professional help.

B. Are other things not helping?

You've tried massage, exercise, yoga, wilderness adventures, herbs, and a women's book club, and you still feel lousy. We congratulate you for doing all these things for yourself. Don't stop. But get some professional help.

C. Are your problems chronic?

Everyone feels blue at times, and we all have bad days. But if you have been waiting months or years for a good day, that is not normal. You deserve to feel better, and if you haven't been able to achieve this for yourself, don't consider this a failure. Just make sure that you get some professional help.

IV. Selecting the right therapist.

A. Do you have such severe symptoms that you feel you might need medication?

If you have symptoms such as insomnia, loss of appetite, no interest in ordinary activities, terrible feelings of depression or hopelessness, panic attacks, or fear of leaving your house, you may have a condition that responds well to medications. You might consider seeing a psychiatrist; a psychiatrist specializes in prescribing medications as well as in psychotherapy. It is important to add that while many primary care physicians are well aware of the effectiveness of psychiatric medications and prescribe them regularly, this is not their area of expertise. If the first medical treatment doesn't work, don't think you are incurable. Consult with a psychiatrist.

B. Is it okay to ask for referrals?

If you don't have friends who are in therapy and don't know who to ask, then skip this part. But people do get reputations for their specialization. See whether you can find someone who is very pleased with the work of a particular therapist. That therapist may not turn out to be the right person for you, but at least you have started out with someone who is known to be good.

C. Should you interview more than one therapist?

This can be time-consuming and expensive, and you want to get started with someone once you have made the decision to get help. But assuming you can manage it, it can be helpful to see more than one person, to get a feel for how different people work. You can ask questions about the particular therapist's theoretical framework, techniques, usual length of treatment, how they handle vacations, payment, phone calls, anything. This is going to be your therapy. It's important to be informed.

D. Do you go with your gut?

After all is said and done, you have to feel safe and comfortable with your therapist. You will have to work to build up real trust, and you might as well have everything going for you at the outset. Trust your inner self. If you like this person and sense he would make an ideal partner and ally on your journey, you've made a good start.

V. Use the program to stay on track.

A. Do you know what your goals are?

If you don't know where you want to go, how do you know whether you're aiming in the right direction? Your goals for therapy, for changing, have to be more specific than "I want to feel better." That's a beginning, a signal that you need to do something, but it's not a goal.

Use Chapter Seven, "Achievable Goals for Therapy," to clarify exactly what you are working on. When things feel fuzzy, slow, or confusing, review your goals. Then you can redirect your energy to get back on track. Or it may be time to redefine your goals.

B. Are you staying clear about the therapy relationship?

As therapy progresses, so does the relationship with the therapist. Generally, it becomes more intimate, more important, more trusting. It is within this safe, trusting, and valuable relationship that much of the work of therapy gets done.

As the relationship grows and develops, you have more opportunity to use it to work through old traumas and hurts, to reshape your view of the world, and to establish a clear and comfortable sense of yourself. However, this healing relationship is not a passive one in which the mere presence of the therapist changes you. It is what you do and how you change within that relationship that is the important work of therapy. Stay clear about who your therapist is to you. Work on the issues in Chapter Four, "The Relationship Trap," to make sure that the therapy relationship really works for you.

C. Are you keeping your finger on the pulse of your treatment?

Don't stay stuck in your work. Use the guide in Chapter Five, "Five Warning Signs That You're Wasting Your Time," to stay on top of things. Are you keeping secrets? You can do something about that. Have you idealized your therapist in such a way that you find yourself wanting to impress him or her rather than be vulnerable? You can get your therapist to help you with this.

Be active. You are the agent of change.

D. Use the Chart.

If you do this, you will stay on track. Every one of the issues we are describing here is somewhere in the chart. If you are idealizing your therapist, for example, you are in a fantasy on the left side of the chart, and you will continue to feel inadequate and powerless. You need to deal with the reality of your therapist's imperfection and the feelings of fear and disappointment you have about that. This may remind you of your disappointment in your parents. Begin to grieve that, and you are on your way.

Or you may be on a downward spiral toward the bottom of a familiar pit, where you feel hopeless and worthless. This is a position on the bottom left. It means you have gotten reattached to a fantasy on the upper left. Can you identify what it is? Has something real happened to you that you are afraid you can't deal with? Something has caused you to revert to your old defenses. Think about your bad feelings as old feelings, old defensive patterns, rather than as the truth about today's reality and the reality about you. Working in this way to separate your past from your present, your defensive reactions from your true self will gradually show you the way out of the pit.

At first you will need to draw the chart each time you use it. Soon, however, you will be able to use the process in your head to help yourself quickly, spontaneously, and effectively.

VI. Stick with therapy when the resistance comes.

A. Do you recognize your resistance?

Resistance is a natural response to change. Because we instinctively want to maintain the status quo, making things different takes energy and work. You're going to get tired. Eventually, when the changes start to come, and they feel good, they will have a pull of their own, motivating you to move forward. Even so, we tend to want to do things the same old way.

Resistance can take countless forms: boredom, anger, getting sidetracked, and attachment to old defensive patterns. Learn to recognize what you do that keeps you in one place. This is a great topic for discussion in your therapy. Your therapist can usually see it better than you can, and he or she will be happy to help you learn to see it for yourself.

B. Are you giving yourself a break?

We all have our limits. Are you pushing yourself too hard? Do you actually need to take a break from your work? Sometimes you need to let some changes sink in for a while, or you need to practice some new behaviors before you can move forward.

You may be apprehensive about moving to the next step. If that is the case, it is important to be willing to face some new pain. Your resistance may be about avoiding the bottom right of the chart. Remember to pace yourself; getting overwhelmed serves no purpose. But push yourself a little. You will find out whether you can handle it, and you probably can. Have faith in yourself—move forward!

A Little at a Time

One last reminder about how we face real pain. We do it in small increments, as much at a time as we can tolerate. We have to take special care of ourselves when doing this work. The pain is real, and so we need real, soothing things to help. Sometimes that means connection with close friends and loved ones. Sometimes it means special things for you, things that you know will make you feel better—nurturing things, treats, a good diet, enough sleep, and exercise.

There is no value in being overwhelmed by feelings, though there is value in allowing yourself to be embraced by them. As children, we may have learned that we couldn't cope with the pain. As adults, we have to learn something new: that we can. Step by step, as we live through the pain, we learn that we don't have to run away from it into destructive defensive fantasies. Grieving happens, little by little, bit by bit. But it happens.

Like the women in this book, you may have great pain to face in coming to terms with your past. But the rewards are greater than the pain: when you are not using your energy to support the fantasies of the past, you can find yourself as the unique, loving, productive, and creative person that you can be.

And the day came when the risk to remain tight in a bud was more painful than the risk it took to blossom.

Anaïs Nin

Suggested Reading

Dowling, Collette. *The Cinderella Complex.* New York: Summit Books, 1981.

Eichenbaum, Luise, and Orbach, Susie. *Understanding Women.* New York: Basic Books, 1983.

Friday, Nancy. *My Mother, My Self.* New York: Delacorte Press, 1977.

Gilligan, Carol. *In a Different Voice.* Cambridge, Mass: Harvard University Press, 1982.

Herman, Judith. *Trauma and Recovery.* New York: Basic Books, 1992.

Jordan, Judith, et al. Women's Growth in Connection: Writings from the Stone Center. New York: Guilford Press, 1991.

Lerner, Harriet. *The Dance of Anger.* New York: Harper and Row, 1985.

Miller, Alice. *Prisoners of Childhood.* New York: Basic Books, 1981.

Miller, Jean Baker. *Toward a New Psychology of Women.* Boston: Beacon Press, 1986.

Shapiro, Joan. *Men: A Translation for Women.* New York: Dutton, 1982.

Stern, Ellen Sue. *The Indispensable Woman.* New York, Toronto: Bantam Books, 1988.

Tatelbaum, Judy. *The Courage to Grieve.* New York: Lippincott and Crowell, 1980.

Index